My Nightmare in Georgia

Based on a True Story

By A. L. Norton

Table of Contents

Prologue

I have a story to tell. Knowing that you aren't supposed to go through life dwelling on the past, I do it anyway. Why? Because I relive it every single day of my life. Certain smells, certain things people say or do, many things on any day, can become a flashback or a trigger.

Not going to sugarcoat anything while writing my story. Having received a lot of rude comments from family members about revealing my story, all I have to say is, "I am not ashamed of myself for revealing my story." They should be ashamed of being embarrassed by me, revealing what happened to me to the world. People like them cause women and children not to get help when being sexually abused, abused, or raped. They keep it a secret because they feel as if they will humiliate their family, or even themselves. Or maybe it will get brushed under the rug, and the court system will fail you, like what happened to me. What happens if nobody believes you?

So many emotions flow through you when something terrible happens to you. Isolation and loneliness become the first emotions to step forward and show their ugly faces. Then come the bitterness and anger, and not just at your attacker.

You're angry at the world. Screw everyone. Then comes sadness, depression, anxiety, phobias—and your attacker is walking around free of worries, enjoying his freedom, living life to the fullest and looking for another life to damage and destroy. We have such an incredible justice system, don't we? They failed me terribly as a child, and I will forever live bitter and angry about it. Even though my attacker had already committed the crime and I was not his first victim, he walked. It was a kick to the face. Guess what? He repeated the offense over and over, leaving a trail of destroyed lives in his path. The justice system could have prevented that. But it was his word against mine. What the hell happened to the polygraph tests? As I sat shivering from being a horrified teenager, sitting next to my younger siblings in the police station after CPS (Child Protective Services) rescued us, I wondered if they would polygraph us, so they knew I was telling the truth. I prayed they would.

As they separated my brother from my sister and me, taking us to protective custody, I kept my fingers crossed and hoped they would bring out the polygraph. He was a liar. I was telling the truth. He was expecting me to live my life holding secrets that burned inside of me. All of his dirty secrets. The violence that he allocated was becoming more intense. Would I live to tell the secrets that were burning inside of me? I wasn't sure how long I was going to remain around to find out. There may be some dull moments in my story, but make sure you read it from beginning to end. If I could go back in time, knowing what my future would hold for me, I would have never leaped into the U-Haul truck that one summer day with dad and traveled back to Georgia. Everyone has a story, some good ones, some bad ones. Some tell them, and some keep them locked away inside themselves forever. They expected me to do just that. My name is Lindsey; here is my story.

Chapter One
Going Home

It was the summer of 1990, and the cicadas were making themselves known. All the outdoors sounded like electricity, even though our home was in a small town. We had crummy television reception because mom was a single mom and couldn't afford cable. Hence, the only way I could sit and stare like an idiot was to squat on the chipped paint off the front porch and pass my eyes over the cornfields across the street and listen to the cicadas. That's what I did when I wanted to wonder and lose myself in a mental coma.

My mom gave a shout for me from somewhere inside the house, and I turned to face the screen-in front door. I couldn't see inside because it was daylight out, and the place was dimly lit. But I rolled my eyes for her, just in case she could see me. Then I turned my eyes back to the fields and wondered it again. Would my dad keep his promise for a change? Would he show up from Georgia to pick my brother, sister, and me up?

They're questions you might ask when your parents are two years divorced on account of dad beating you up all the time and then trying to end things by attempting to set the entire house on fire with the family in it while they are sleeping. So, what if he whooped us and was mean to us?

So, what if we went to school covered in bruises or had an untreated broken bone?

Or sometimes was too scared to go home? Mom had moved us to Indiana, where all of our families lived, and it just wasn't 'home' to me. Georgia was my home. My friends were there. My school was there. It was where I wanted to be.

Since my parent's divorce, my dad had become much more pleasant to us kids. In the back of my mind, I had concealed the fact that when I was eleven, and my mom left in a hurry in the middle of the night to escape his abuse and trying to burn us alive, he called and tricked me into telling him that mom was alone at my grandparent's house. He snuck in through the unlocked front door, placed a gun to her head, and kidnapped her. The neighbors watched her being dragged, screaming, and pleading for her life down the driveway. One neighbor called the police in terror, as she continued to plea for her life. He drove her through the countryside and threatened to kill her, pistol-whipped her, beat her, then threw her out of the car at the local Dairy Queen. Seeing the black and blue swelling all over her face terrified me. I felt sorry for her. She slept with a knife and a baseball bat in fear that he would come back. He ran like a coward back to Georgia, so the police never got him. And here I was, bags packed, with a promise that he would never hit us again, heading back to Georgia to live with him. Every car that passed around the corner, I stretched my twelve-year-old neck to see if it was him. Nope.

I still sat there and wondered and listened because my dad was excellent at breaking his word. My fingers crept up by instinct to feel for the silver necklace that hung there, sometimes ignored, but never forgotten, and never taken off. A best friend necklace my dad bought me when I was eleven. After my parents divorced when I was eleven, and all the craziness settled down, mom had to move back to Georgia to move into the house we had lived in for approximately seven years, sell it, and complete some things before our permanent move back to Indiana. I would leave my friends and yet another school once again. That's what happens when your dad is in the Army. You get settled somewhere and then it is time to move again. It was hard to have stability and make and keep friends. I hated always being the new girl in school. I wasn't always accepted either.

Dad took me shopping at the mall while we were down there and bought the necklace for me. I wore one half, and he wore the other, so I thought.

Funny how you can love a parent after taking so many beatings from them, be mistreated by them, observe them mistreating your whole family, and forgive them. There were good times, but the troubled times outweighed the good. He had an innovative way of getting into your head and thinking he was the greatest man on earth. Master manipulator.

I'm thinking narcissist.

A bit of orange swept just above the grasses across my distance, then slowed as a U-Haul made its way carefully around a sharp curve in the road. I hopped to my feet and turned to the door, shouting, "he's here, mom!" Grabbing a bag, I swung it over my shoulder, then picked up a box off the front porch and ran down the steps, grinning from ear to ear. Only a few weeks left before my freshman year started in high school, and I wasn't wasting any time getting back to Georgia to spend the rest of summer with my friends. Mom met me back on the porch as I grabbed the last of my belongings, and she dabbed me on my shoulder. Stopping and staring, we locked eyes. "Lindsey, are you sure you want to go?" Her eyes turned to worry as she glanced over at the U-Haul truck and the man stepping out of it.

"Yes, mom. I want to go. He made a promise; he'll keep it; I am sure of it. Besides, I don't like it here; it doesn't feel like home," I replied in a firm tone. You could still see the worry and some panic in her eyes and facial expression. "Mom, I will be okay. I will monitor the other two," I reassured her.

A sharp, energized voice broke our moment. "Hey, we need to get moving and get on the road," dad beamed a magnificent smile as if everything was right in the world, and for now, it was. The cicadas had reminded me all afternoon about that other world, the electric world, and with my dad carrying me off there, I was pretty sure things were going to be alright.

"Where's your brother and sister at, kiddo? You the only one going?" Turning towards the old beige vinyl-sided house.

"I'll run inside and get them." Swinging the front door open, I hollered for my two younger siblings to hustle it up. They came sprinting out the front door, arms loaded full of their belongings. I didn't want them to go back to Georgia with my dad and me. But they just had to go, too. Whatever big sister does, the younger girls must follow along. We gave mom one last kiss and hug goodbye, then raced to the U-Haul truck and jumped in. The two youngest, Jake, ten years old, and Jessica, seven-years-old, sat in the middle. I sat next to the door to make sure neither of them would fall out. I was protective of them even though they continuously worked my last nerve, but that's what siblings do.

Dad slid in the driver's side of the U-Haul, and the smell of gasoline lingered in the cab's front as he stuck the key in the ignition and fired up the engine. Glancing over at him, I reminisced when I lived with him approximately six months prior. It only lasted maybe a month and a half. Dad picked me up and drove me back to Georgia by myself to live with him. Unknowingly, he lived in a small two-bedroom apartment that was gross, and you could barely move or breathe in. The school I had to go to was within walking distance. You could see it out the back window of our apartment, and I was the only white student. Thank God the kids didn't bother me. It was frightful. I was living with dad's new girlfriend and her two young sons in the small apartment. God, I couldn't stand it. Zach was two years old, and Jason was only six months.

Zach slept in a crib in dad's girlfriend, Tina, and dad's room, while Zach slept in a crib in my small space you could barely walk through. He cried in the middle of the night, keeping me awake, making it hard for me to get up and go to school. I was late or too tired to go. The living arrangements were so terrible I just had dad send me back home on a plane to Indiana. It bummed me it didn't work out. One thing was for sure, dad wasn't mean, and he didn't hit me. So, I trusted to move back to Georgia with him.

I was more than eager to get back to Columbus, Georgia, my home, where I belonged. Glancing over at dad as he put the U-Haul in the drive, his deep brown hair was thinner than the last time I saw him. He was getting a receding hairline. His teeth were stained yellow from all the years of his smoking habit, and something about his mahogany eyes didn't set well with me. As the U-Haul pulled out of the driveway, I saw mom fade away in the rear-view mirror. My heart sank. I had a lump in my throat, and butterflies fluttered in my little thirteen-year-old tummy. I felt kind of as if my skin went pale, as if something wasn't right. Was this a bad idea? A mistake?

Staring out the side of the window, watching the moving trees, with the window down and the humid wind blowing in my face, I thought about my friends and all the great times and memories we were going to make together.

Shaking off the horrible feeling that had gripped onto me, I lay my head back and prepared myself for the long thirteen-hour trip home. Little did I know that this move with my dad would be a tremendous mistake I would ever make and alter my life forever.

Chapter Two
Home Sweet Home

Making that thirteen-hour drive was tiresome. My butt hurt, and my legs were numb. My shoulder ached from my sister leaning her head against it through most of the trip while sleeping. There was a wet spot on my sleeve where she drooled! Oh well. I yawned and stretched while smiling at the beautiful surroundings that I was all too familiar with back home in Columbus, Georgia.

Dad pulled the U-Haul up to an apartment complex. It appeared to be one of his military barracks. He was a drill sergeant in the Army. Seeing the apartments and passing them many times before, I had never really been on the inside. Praying they appeared better than they viewed from the outside, we jumped out of the U-Haul, stretched, and followed dad so he could show us around before we transferred our belongings into our new home if you wanted to call it that.

We were on the third floor, so we trudged up the stairs. After a thirteen-hour drive, my skinny legs were about to give out. Dad unlocked the door, and we strolled inside. Sweet Jesus. It was all I could think of as I looked at the apartment. The floor was white ceramic tile, the type you see in school lunchrooms. In the living room, there was a broken-down brown leather couch that had seen better days. Dad must have brought it home from the barracks, or maybe picked it up from a Goodwill or dumpster. And the kitchen had a round table that wobbled, which probably had come from the same place as the couch, and the chairs stained all to hell and didn't match. No pictures were hanging on the walls, just bare drywall with a poor paint job.

As we walked down the hall, straight ahead was the master bedroom, and to the right were two other rooms. My sister and I had to share one room, and my brother had his room. Both were tiny, and dad had those fold-out, roll away beds in each room (you know, the ones you see in hotels?) for us with those itchy green military blankets on our beds. I went and lay on my bed and had about thirty springs plunge into my back. My sister and I giggled but made sure dad didn't hear us. She left the room to get her belongings to bring them in. I stood up and took a glance around. I felt as if this apartment had been hurried. Dad knew for over a month that we were coming. Why didn't he take more time to make a home for us? If mom had seen this, she would have us put our belongings back in the car and make us come back to Indiana. That was one thing mom didn't tolerate, us kids living in filthy, unfit conditions. Dad was clean in some ways, but not in others. I guess I blew it off because I thought that at least he was trying. I figured I could eventually help dad clean up and decorate. He said the apartment was only temporary, anyway. Dad called out for me to come to get my belongings. It was getting late, and he had to have the U-Haul back by morning. Walking out of my room and trudging back down the dreaded stairs.

The stairs were killing my legs, turning them to jelly. When I was finally through, I could have done a victory dance if my legs hadn't hurt so badly. Staring at the crackerjack box called "my room," I started unpacking, starting with my stereo first. I have an immense amount of love for music and can't survive without it. Slipping in my Aerosmith tape, I turned it up just enough to get my blood flowing and energized to get my tasks of getting my room together done. It took about an hour. I had little to unpack, which was okay by me. Glancing over at my sister, she had done her part of unpacking and settling in. She didn't do too badly for a seven-year-old. She was proud of herself. Secretly, I smiled.

We were all tired, so dad cooked grilled cheese and tomato soup for dinner. We ate quickly and then hurried off to bed. Although I was quite tired,

I couldn't fall asleep. I lay there in bed, with my radio turned on at a low volume. I always slept with my radio on low. Dad peeked his head in my room and told me that before I left the next day to make sure Tina was here first to watch my brother and sister. My mouth gaped. Thank God it was dark in my room, and he didn't see my facial expression. He wouldn't have liked it one bit. "Okay," I politely answered. So far, he was doing well at trying to be excellent. I wasn't about to blow it with a crappy attitude. I just hoped to hell the winch didn't weasel her way to move in here with us. I had a huge dislike for her since she moved right in to my parents' house not long after my mom had fled from his abuse. It was mom's house. Not Tina's. Tina tried though and I smiled the day mom had to get her out of there. Tina attempted to load up things that belonged to mom and as mom snatched them from her, I giggled - just a little.

Besides, there wasn't any room. I heard the bedroom door shut, then glanced over to see that my sister was already sound asleep. Still tossing and turning, I couldn't sleep if my life depended on it. I didn't know whether it was the excitement of being able to see my friends finally the next day or the thirty-five freaking springs from the mattress poking into my back. Bet my money it was the fucking springs.

Chapter Three
Hello Friends

The sun illuminated streams of light through the cracks of the dark brown sheet; dad hung over my bedroom window as a temporary curtain until he could purchase one. I knew damn well that sheet was not brief as cheap as dad was. The kids were already up, watching cartoons and playing, and I could hear Tina's voice, which made me cringe and scrunch my face in disgust.

Rolling to my side and pulling myself out of bed, she was the last issue I wanted to deal with on my first day back home. I was rubbing my somnolent eyes; my heart raced as I thought about the fact that today was the day I would see my close friends again. Joy blossomed within me. It was such a wonderful feeling.

Patty, Sherry, Courtney, and I were always together. We shared a wonderful and exciting friendship, full of laughter and fun. We got into a lot of trouble together, too. We were each other's friends, therapists, a shoulder to lean on, and had wiped each other's tears. We shared secrets and trusted each other. We shared a bond that could not be broken. Friends like that are so hard to find.

They were a vital part of my life. Hell, they were my life.

We dressed a little provocatively and always had our hair and makeup done, but we climbed trees, splashed through the creek, and loved anything you could do outdoors. We were tomboys at heart. The girls and I loved to sit around and babble on about our dreams when we grew up. I wanted to be an author, dancer, or maybe even an actress. The possibilities are endless, right? I was a real drama queen. I think I still am to this day.

Tip toeing down the hallway, I glanced around, looking for the phone. It was hanging on a thin wall between the kitchen and the living room. Shit! She is going to see me. I thought to myself.

Wondering over to the phone, picking it up quickly, and dialing Courtney's number, I could hear Tina speak to me in the background. "Well, hey there, Lindsey."

"Hey, Tina." I turned back around. "Winch," I mumbled.

When I spoke with Courtney, she could not withhold her excitement that I was back home, either. She agreed to call the other girls and tell them I was back. We were to meet at a creek that we loved to hang out. Behind the old neighborhood that I used to live in before my dad became a psychopath and tried to broil us all, and we had to move. It was hidden away from society and quiet. We had a rope tied to a tree, where you could swing and drop into the water. A lot of partying took place down there, and we were the culprits that threw them. Many of our guy friends would join us. We would laugh and have so much fun until our cheeks and jaws ached. We had built and were continuing to create some glorious memories there.

Dashing to my closet, I pulled out a pink tank tight tank top and short jean shorts, then raced for the shower. Quickly, I got dressed after my shower and blew my long, dish blonde hair dry, and straightened it. I threw on some make-up, then glanced at myself in my vanity mirror. I was of slender build and finally filling out and to get a bit of a figure that I was proud of. Throwing on my white canvas tennis shoes, I sprinted for the door before hearing the most annoying voice stop me. "Where are you going? And where are you going dressed like that?" Tina strolled into the living room with her hands on her hips as if she owned my birthrights.

"Dad knows where I am going, and you did not give birth to me. Bye." I gave a devilish grin and strolled out the front door. Trudging down the three flights of stairs and out the apartment complex door, I ran in the muggy air, you can almost cut it with a knife, Georgia humidity and heat, and towards the old neighborhood, between the two houses that led to the creek. Hurdling over quite a few bushes, sliding down some rocks, and scooting down an embankment, I finally made it! And there they were, waiting for me. We were all smiles and laughter.

My heart thumped against my chest with joy as I dashed through the creek water to get to the other side to hug them all. Sherry passed me a beer. Yes, I was thirteen and drinking a beer, so what? We thought we were cool, but now that I look back on it, we weren't. We still had fun without it.

Sitting along the embankment with our toes in the cool creek water, in the hot Georgia sun, we caught up on our lives, and the girls caught me up on all the affairs I had missed out on. I was jealous of all the excitement that took place while I was stuck in "The Land of Nowhere."

Stumbling home, I went inside, saying a prayer to the heavens above that nobody noticed I was three sheets to-the-wind drunk. Walking in the front door, the first person to be seen is Tina, sitting on the couch.

"Where's dad," I questioned in a soft tone.

"He's in the kitchen," she replied sarcastically.

Rolling my eyes, striding past her, I came upon the kitchen. Sitting down at the kitchen table to have dinner with dad and the four of the five kids, dad gave me "the look."

"Where have you been?" he questioned firmly while taking a bite of his mashed potatoes.

"I was at Patty's all day," I smiled, trying to play it cool.

"Hope you don't think you're going to be running the streets all day," he remarked, staring me in the eyes.

"Oh, I know," I pleasantly agreed.

Glancing over at Tina, she was smirking as I was getting a lecture. "What are you looking at?" I asked her with annoyance. Before I could even think, dad backhanded me across the face, almost knocking me out of the chair. Tina's eyes bulged, and the kids stopped eating deafening silence entered the room.

My lip quivered, my heart sank into my stomach, and I shuddered uncontrollably. Dad didn't hit kids and women like kids and women. He hit us like he would another man. But dad would never hit another man. He was a coward. He preferred to bully and beat women and children. At least, that is how I saw it. I once heard someone say, "Once you hit a woman, you are no longer a man." Guess my dad was just a pussy. I hope to this day that he is ashamed of himself, but probably not. Sitting at the dinner table, I fought so hard not to cry. We could not cry. Every time my eyes filled with tears, I rolled them to the back of my head to make the water go back down. It was rough. I was too scared to move. I didn't even pick my fork up to eat. My face burned. Heat rose off my flesh like a flame of fire had been lit on it. He would strike you in the head and face; your ears would ring and have a burning sensation.

Damn, why did he have to hit? Why couldn't he keep his hands to himself? He hurt not only me physically, but he hurt me mentally. I know physical pain hurts and heals, but it is the mental and emotional pain that sticks with you forever. It hurts you the most. The bastard broke his promise. If you can't trust your parent, who do you trust? Hoping that I had not made the wrong choice of coming back to live with dad lingered in my mind.

I am a migraine sufferer, and dad hitting me in the face caused my head to hurt. I excused myself from the table and went to my room to lie in my bed. He let me leave the table without eating.

All my life, he had abused continuously me, my brother, and my mom. He never harmed my sister. I was the primary target. Mom once told me that my abuse started when I was just an infant. He would toss me like a football into a bedroom when I cried too much, shut the door, block it, and dare her to go in after me. It broke her heart, and she would cry. He left tons of bruises over the years, and even once, he broke my tailbone just because I left my skateboard on my bedroom floor. When I was seven years old, I was not too fond of ravioli. Dad made me sit at the table until I ate every bite. It was tough swallowing it, and I gagged when it went down my throat. I ended up throwing it up back into the bowl.

He made me eat my vomit.

My brother, when he was six years old, spilled Kool-Aid on the brand-new carpet. He took my brother to his room and beat him in his face until it was swollen and black and blue. I sat on the couch in the den, hearing my brother being thrown against closet doors and walls, screaming. I wet myself. I was so frightened that dad was going to kill him. I prayed so hard that my brother would be okay. I wanted to help him, but I was only nine years old. What could I do? I still, to this day, have horrific flashbacks of that day.

Dad would do cruel things to pets, too. He would surprise us with a new cat or dog, allow us to become emotionally attached to them. We would come home from school one day, and they would be gone with no explanation. My siblings and I were left with broken hearts and no answers. Minding our own business was best for us.

Still, to this very day, I believe he is the maniac that poisoned my German Shepard. I found him with his face floating in his water bowl one morning before school. It was devastating. I threw myself on the ground, screaming and crying for my mom while holding his lifeless body. He was only a year old. Later, mom found a little black bag in the backyard. She had never seen it before. I know the heartless bastard had something to do with it. As upset as I was, I couldn't believe they still made me attend school that day. It was hard to concentrate and not think about my poor dog. That was my ninth birthday present. It took everything I had not to burst into tears. I just wanted to go home.

My parents waited to bury him after I got home from school that day to say my one last goodbye. We wrapped him in my favorite blanket. After we buried him, my family went into the house; I stayed out by the fresh dirt my dog was lying beneath. The backyard was empty when I was so used to coming home and running straight out here to run and play "chase each other" with him. Hot tears streamed down my cheeks, and I used my sleeve to wipe them off along with my runny nose. I sat there for a long time, almost until dark. Even after we buried my dog and all the cruel, and hateful shit dad to me, for some God forsaken reason, I still loved that son of a bitch.

Chapter Four
Is It Happening Again

The ringing of the phone woke me up the next morning. Damn near tripped over my feet as my legs were tangled up in that "itchy as hell green military blanket" on my springy ass bed.

Sliding down the hallway on the dirty ceramic white tile that may have been mopped twice since we moved into the shithole apartment, I made it to the phone by the fourth ring and answered. My voice was raspy since I had just awoken. "Hello?"

"Hey, girl. It's Courtney," she announced, like it was the first time I had ever heard her voice and hadn't a clue who she was. "Hey," I replied, leaning one foot against the wall, taking the long phone cord and wrapping some of it around my finger. (Kids today don't know the struggle with talking on the phone back then.)

"Calling to see if you want to hang out today."

"You up for it?"

Pausing and thinking for a moment about what happened the previous night and the hard smack across my face that I took from dad, I didn't know if I should even call him at work and ask him if I could leave the house. But I decided I was going to grow a set of balls and go for it. "Yes. Let me call and ask my dad. I am sure it will be okay. Give me an hour to call him, get myself ready, and meet me halfway, okay?"

"Sounds good," she responded cheerfully. Hanging up with Courtney, my fingers were almost reluctant to dial dad's work number to question if I could go to Courtney's. Tina had the kids out and about, and I was the only home, so I was hoping he would just give me the okay. It took everything I had to dial that number, and when he answered, I almost just hung up the phone. "Staff Sargeant Smith, how may I help you?" His voice was so deep and firm.

"Dad, it's me. I have a question." Beads of sweat formed on my forehead.

"Yeah, go ahead."

"Can I go to Courtney's?" Now I was ready to pass out.

Silence.

Okay, maybe this was a bad idea to ask. (Rolls eyes)

"Sure. Go ahead. Be home by 5 p.m."

"Thank you." I politely replied.

He hung up the phone, and I released the air from my lungs and caught my breath. Damn, asking him for anything was like planning your funeral.

Rushing to get myself ready, I did the usual, showering and picking out my clothing. When sitting down at the vanity mirror to apply my makeup...there it was, what I had seen so many times before. A bruised handprint across my face, up to my cheekbone.

Being kind of pro from hiding the bruises went a thick layer of foundation and facial powder and prayer that nobody noticed. They taught us as children to keep our hands to ourselves; maybe they should have classes to teach grown-ups to do the same.

Courtney's house was twenty minutes away from my apartment. We always walked and met halfway, then back to Courtney's hanging out. She had her room, which meant privacy since I had to share my room with my sister.

Courtney was wildly infatuated with boys.

Me, not so much; I didn't trust them.

Wonder why? I compared them all to my dad; I think. Having a lot of guy friends was one thing, but having a boyfriend? I wasn't too fanatical about that. I guess I believed they were all the same. They hit, they hurt, and they mistreat you. I wanted no more of that in my life! All Courtney did was talk about boys. She always had a boyfriend. Once she broke up with one, she had another one by the next day. No sooner than did I approach her, she noticed the handprint bruise on my face. Guess it was that bad and noticeable. We turned toward her house and strolled. "Does it hurt?" she asked curiously.

My head glanced over at her. Courtney was shorter than me. I was 5'7, and she was 5'6. She was curvier than I was and had shoulder-length blonde hair with brown eyes. A dazzling white crooked smile that the older high school boys seemed to love. Nodding my head, "Yes. It hurts. But it doesn't only just physically hurt, but emotionally as well." My eyes filled with water, but I was quick to fight back the tears. I was becoming a pro at it. Courtney shook her head in disapproval of what my dad had done. She knew he had done this so many times before. "You should tell someone," she suggested in a soft tone.

"No. No, Courtney, I can't," I replied bluntly. "They will send my dad to jail and me back to Indiana. Mom and I don't get along. I can't go back. Besides, you are here, not there," I panicked a little at her suggestion.

"Well, I'd rather see you safe than beaten on all the time," she spoke with concern.

I stopped walking and turned towards her. "If dad hits me again, I will tell someone. Until then, it's our secret, okay?"

She folded her arms and took a deep breath.

"Okay."

There was an elementary school across the street from where we were standing. Walking over to the playground, we snatched up a swing and sat down, twirling, swinging, and dragging our feet around in the dirt below, where there once was a patch of grass. We babbled on for a while, with me forcing a laugh and faking a smile here and there. I was not okay. Suddenly, I didn't feel like hanging out anymore; I just wanted to go home, if that is what you wanted to call it.

Courtney and I parted ways, and I don't think I glanced up one time on my twenty-minute walk home. Usually, I was daydreaming about something, but the entire time my mind was completely blank.

Opening the door to the main entrance to the apartment building we lived in, my feet took the first steps up the staircase when I heard a woman and my dad laughing. It came from the first-floor apartment to my left. The smell of freshly baked chocolate chip cookies filled the air, and so did the sound of children's laughter. "Dad must have found him a new woman," I thought. "Wonder if Tina knows," I giggled. Then I continued up the stairs.

I cooked my brother and sister dinner that night, made them take baths, and got them to bed. Tina never showed up with her two young boys, not that I was complaining. Dad stayed down in the first-floor apartment wasn't complaining about that either. It was peaceful in the apartment. I stayed awake a little longer and did some much-needed cleaning. I hated my siblings for having to live in such filth. I made sure that their clothing was washed and dried, seems how the adults didn't make it a point to make sure the kids had clean clothes to wear. That night made me realize that monitoring my brother and sister would have to happen more often and be a priority. I could handle myself. I just wished they would have stayed back in Indiana with mom. It would have made dealing with dad a lot easier, or so I thought.

Chapter Five
Starting High School

The school was fast approaching, and my nerves were getting the best of me. High school meant kids older than me.

Dad was acting eerie. He would go to the neighbor ladies' apartment downstairs during the day when he wasn't at work or when Tina wasn't around, and then was home in the apartment when Tina was around. Then, Tina kept calling dad Mike. His name was Charles. Not Mike. Curiously, I wanted to know why she and her family called him Mike, but I was too afraid to ask.

So, I just kept wondering, hoping to find out the truth. I figured it would come out eventually.

Dad took us school shopping a few days before school started. He was so damned cheap with clothing. I passed on the K-Mart clothes. My sister always followed in my footsteps, so she did too. I wished she wouldn't have because she needed jeans desperately. My brother didn't give a crap. He would wear anything. I got my supplies, though, knowing I would never use the son-of-a-bitches.

I was not too fond of school. I had a learning disability; I am pretty sure of it. I was always the kid that walked around with the red mark on their forehead from sleeping in class. The high school I would attend would be a little rough around the edges, but I knew what I was getting myself into when I came back to Georgia. Somehow, I would get through it. I just hoped that the hard smack across the face was just a onetime incident.

The night before school started, I tossed and turned in my bed as each darned spring from the roll-out-bed mattress stabbed me in the back and jabbed me in my rig cage. God, I wanted an actual bed. I missed my waterbed back home in Indiana. The last time my eyes glanced at the small black alarm clock on the ceramic-tiled floor next to me, it was 1:45 a.m. Being able to wake up at 6 a.m. would be hell not being a morning person, anyway.

Rolling over once again, clearing my mind of any thoughts, I finally fell into a deep slumber. The alarm clock clamored in my ear at precisely 6 a.m.

Didn't I just fall asleep?

Rubbing my somnolent eyes, feeling weary and sluggish from not enough sleep, I knew how dad was about school and being on time so; I dragged myself out of bed and hurried my feet across the floor like a zombie, all the way to the bathroom to get a quick shower. Returning to my room, I sifted through my closet and picked out a blue jean skirt and pink blouse to go with my white canvas shoes. Everyone always complimented how nice and toned my legs were so, why not show them off? I blew my long hair dry and curled it. I applied some nice make-up and was blessed that the handprint was no longer noticeable. I then gave myself a little smile. Someone always bullied me at school, and it was just one reason I hated having to go. I had to deal with being bullied at home and dealing with being bullied, hit, beaten, and emotionally abused by your dad? Having to deal with mental stress every day was unbearable for a kid. But my friends always stuck up for me and had my back when things weren't going right for me.

That's why I loved them so much.

Standing up and gazing into the vanity mirror, turning side to side, I had improved significantly on the way I applied my makeup and did my hair. Having improved on the way I dressed myself and the fact I had grown into a young woman and fill out over the summer, for once I had just an ounce of self-confidence to walk into that high school that day.

Hearing a whimper, I turned over to see my sister struggling to get herself ready for school, too. She was having a hell of a time getting her jeans to fasten, so I went over to help, completely forgetting that dad thought that after you turned a year-old, you should be able to do things on your own. What a schmuck. "You need new jeans," I told her as I finally got her button fastened. "But you said you wouldn't get caught dead in K-Mart jeans, Lindsey." She peered at me with her big blue eyes and those cute little freckles that spread across her nose. "Never listen to me," I replied. "Let's go brush and braid your hair. I am running out of time."

Jessica sat down at the vanity mirror and allowed me to braid her long brown hair. Then she put her socks and shoes on. I checked on my brother, who was already waiting in the living room with his backpack. Making Jessica a quick bowl of cereal, I turned to Tina's lazy ass, "Can you get them on the bus. I am going to miss mine?" "Sure." She blew out a puff of cigarette smoke, and I grabbed my backpack and dashed out the front door.

Making it to the bus stop with just a few minutes to spare, other teens were waiting on the big yellow banana as well. It was awkward. It was also an inner-city school, so I was praying to Jesus that I was catching the right school bus. Being too afraid to ask what bus stop it was for, I just figured if I ended up at the wrong school, I would call dad to pick me up and face the freaking wrath! Screeching tires of a big yellow bus came to a halt, and I read the black letter siding. Kendridge High School. Thank God I was on the right bus! Score one thing that went right for the first day of school. Please let the rest of the day keep going well.

The big yellow banana came to a screeching halt in front of the high school. With my face pressed against the window, my eyes bulged, nausea filled my tummy, my heart thumped forcefully against my chest, and I could feel the blood drain from my face, causing me to turn pale white.

There was a half-circled brick wall, standing at about 6 feet that read Kendridge High School, Home of the Bulldogs. Behind it, an enormous building three stories tall. "Holy crap," I mumbled to myself. The high school back in the small town in Indiana was nowhere near this enormous. You could fit that high school into this one and still have plenty of room leftover. My weak, trembling legs rose out of my seat and walked down the aisle, pretending not to be nervous. When I stepped off the very last step and onto the sidewalk, turning and running back home seemed like such a fantastic idea. Taking a deep breath, putting one foot in of the other, I strolled, making my way into the building, straight to the office, and getting my schedule and locker.

Grabbing my schedule, locker code, and number, I wandered up and down the stairs, frantically scanning through the building in search of my locker and classes. Finally found my locker and had a hell of a time opening the damn rusted thing. It took me a lengthy amount of time to find my first two classes, but after that, vexation had taken over me, so I discovered a girl's bathroom and hid there until lunch. Running all over that building had taken its toll on me. I could get quite irritated quickly, which usually would get me into trouble. The girl's bathroom was the best place for me at the moment, needing to get myself back together mentally and emotionally, or the outcome would not have been a good one. Hearing the lunch bell ring, I looked up and thanked the heavens above, snatched up my backpack, and raced to the cafeteria to find my friends. I already knew where it was located. I passed it at least a dozen times while in search of my classrooms. Entering the cafeteria, it was not as huge as I thought it would be. Searching for my friends, we found each other and came up with the great idea of sneaking out the back cafeteria exit and going to hide somewhere outside for a smoke and a chat.

Some of our male friends followed behind. Skipping classes turned into a daily ritual. None of us ended up ever making it to our afternoon classes. We continued to stay hidden out behind the bike racks where we couldn't be seen drinking, smoking, chatting, telling stories, poking fun at one another, making plans for the weekend, and so much laughter. None of us even knew where or had been to an afternoon class ever. I just prayed to God that dad would never find out. One day, our friend Ryan brought a bottle of vodka to school. We smoked cigarettes at the bike racks, drank, got drunk, and walked home. Sherry passed out from being so intoxicated, taking a shortcut through the elementary school playground to reach a wooded area so we couldn't be seen. Sherry and I laughed as we dragged her across the playground to get her out of view. Inside, the school did. She called the police. When they arrived, Courtney begged and pleaded for me to run. She knew what dad could do to me for getting into any trouble. I refused to run and leave all my friends to take the credit for my irresponsible actions. The police called an ambulance for Sherry, and Courtney and I were handcuffed and brought back to the high school. Our punishment was a three-day suspension. They didn't know we had been drinking on school property. They thought we had done it somewhere else. They called our parents to be notified of the situation. Knowing that I was about to face dad for what I had done, chills ran up my spine, and I shuddered in fear. Why did I do stupid things and get into trouble when I knew I had an abusive dad?

Because I was a stupid kid, that's why. Would I ever do something dumb again after what he was about to do to me? Probably. Why? Because I wanted to be a normal teenage kid that does stupid shit. That's why. Free to go. Slowly, I walked home because I knew my dad wasn't picking my ass up. It was a hell of a walk, too. Reaching the apartment building, I opened the door, went in, both legs trembling with dread. I labored my breathing as I opened the front door and observed my dad waiting for my arrival, belt in hand. God, I wanted my mom at this moment.

"Get to your room," he gritted his yellowed teeth together in anger.

So, I walked straight to my room as he commanded. Hearing the pounding sound of his military boots he wore, following behind me, I just wanted to get this over with and prayed it wasn't too bad. We were the only two people home, and it scared the shit out of me. At least if Tina was here, and he got out of control, she could stop him.

Reaching my room, turning around, I peered into his angry eyes. "Pull down your pants," he commanded. So, I did, reluctantly.

"Now pull down your panties, turn around, and lay down on your bed," he commanded again.

Too scared to speak a word, but I thought this was getting nasty. You don't command your developing teenage daughter to pull down her pants and panties. This issue was eerie, abnormal. But what could I do? So, I did what he told me to. Dad uncontrollably beat my ass with a thin belt until he saw blood. Screaming out a few times, he reminded me he would strike me harder and longer if I screamed. I bit my tongue and held my breath, but I couldn't stop myself from crying, and the tears streaming down my cheeks were forming a puddle onto my sheets.

The last strike, he hit me the hardest. Tightening my legs, clenching my toes, I wished someone his size or more prominent would have turned around and done that to him. Make him see how it feels. I would have paid anything to watch it happen. I would sell my soul to the devil to watch dad get one hell of an ass whooping from a bigger man than him. Then maybe he would learn to keep his hands to himself.

After he left the room, I ran my fingers across my bare bottom, then held them in front of me, seeing the blood he had drawn. Who the hell does that to their kid? Pulling my pants up, I lay in my bed and sobbed quietly, so he didn't hear me.

I wanted to sneak past him and call my mom. At least I was safe there. I realized this was a huge mistake. She warned me, but I failed to listen. The jackass was a liar. And I felt like he received some sort of pleasure spanking my bare bottom. He made me very uncomfortable. Something wasn't right. It felt disgusting. You don't see your teenage daughter naked.

As if being bloodied and humiliated with a belt wasn't enough as punishment, I spent the next week unable to leave my room except to shower and go to the bathroom, and I had to have permission to do either. On occasions, dad would make me hold myself for a while before allowing me the privilege of using the bathroom. To top it off, I spent my fourteenth birthday isolated in my room. No cake. No card. No singing the song, "Happy Birthday." No present. Dad made me a cupcake, though. I knew I had done wrong and needed to be punished for it. But dad went way overboard. His punishments were not standard. Indiana and living with mom seemed not-so-bad after all.

Chapter Six

As Long As He Wasn't Hurting The Kids Or Me

Striding into the apartment building entrance, the smell of freshly baked chocolate chip cookies filled the bottom floor's air once again. As a lover of chocolate chip cookies, I knew one when I smelled one! The smell was coming from the apartment that dad had always visited. Standing with one foot on the first step, I debated if I should knock and see who this woman was and what she was like. Then I wondered if dad would be upset if I met her. Screw it. Curiosity got the best of me, so I knocked.

A short, stout woman with black shoulder-length hair and chestnut brown eyes answered the door. She immediately threw me a smile and invited me in. "You must be Lindsey," she chirped.

"Yes. I am Charles' oldest daughter," I smiled.

"I already know. Your dad talks about you, the kids, and I see you pass by the living room window all the time. I am baking chocolate chip cookies. Join me in the kitchen." She led me into the kitchen, where there was a heaping plate full of chocolate chip cookies, and she was pulling out another cookie sheet full out of the oven. She threw some on a plate and handed them to me. "I can already tell that we are going to be great friends," I giggled as I took a bite of the most delicious chocolate chip cookie I had ever tasted in my life.

She babbled on about my dad and how great he was. He was going to leave Tina for her. Katie had no clue what kind of nightmare and bullshit she was getting herself into. Being that she was such a genuine and sweet woman with three small kids of her own, I wished my dad would leave her alone before it got too deep, and she was left empty-handed with broken promises and an empty heart. Besides, she would eventually become a punching bag, anyway.

Katie explained she was newly divorced, and that she had just come out of an abusive relationship. She didn't realize she was possibly going to fall right back into one.

Wanting to warn her, I didn't want to put myself in harm's way, so I just ate the cookies, listened to what she had to say, and kept my mouth shut. I had to live with my dad.

She didn't.

After chatting with Katie, I thanked her for the cookies and left. Walking into our apartment, it wasn't as warm and inviting as Katie's. Strolling into the kitchen where dad was cooking dinner while the kids played, I whispered to dad, "I met Katie."

"You did? What did you think?" he whispered back?

"Two thumbs up and a lot better than Tina," I remarked.

"Really? You think so?" He quizzed.

"Yep! And she can make one hell of a cookie," I quietly giggled.

Dad threw his head back and chuckled

I went to my bedroom and lay on my bed, thinking about how dad played both women. It wasn't right. I knew it wasn't.

I didn't feel bad for Tina, but I did for Katie.

Noticing I had an uneasy feeling when I was around dad, it seemed like something was going on with him I didn't know about. Something he was hiding. Like he was leading two separate lives, but there was more to it. Trying to shake it off and let it go, I couldn't help myself but keep wondering. I guess so long as he wasn't hurting us kids, he could do whatever the hell he wanted. At least, that was what I thought for the moment.

Little did I know, red flags were tossed in front of my face, and soon enough, I was about to find out how evil and wicked my dad had become.

Chapter Seven

A New What

The sound of my bedroom door creaking open awoke me, and dad's voice notified me that Patty was on the phone, sounding rather thrilled. Rolling over to my side, lifting and placing my bare feet on the filthy ceramic floor, I yawned, stood up, pulled my nightgown down, strolled down the hallway to answer the phone. "Hello," I said in a raspy, sleepy voice. "Oh, my God. Girl, I must tell you something," Patty shouted in my ear.

Startled by the sudden shouting, I pulled the phone away from my ear; who needs coffee when you have Patty calling at a little after 9 a.m. on a Saturday.

"Are you still there Lindsey?" she questioned.

"Yes. But I think I am a little deaf in my left ear now. So, what's up?"

"Sorry. Just a little excited. There's a new teen club that opened! Want to go check it out tonight?"

"Sure. You know, I love dancing. What time are you picking me up?" Now I was excited.

"The girls and I will pick you up at 6 p.m. can't wait." She hung up the phone.

Hanging up the phone, dancing at a new teen club sounded terrific! I loved to dance. My only worry was; would dad let me go?

Slowly, playing it cool, I strolled into the kitchen, made myself a cup of coffee, then had a seat at the kitchen table between dad and Tina. They read the morning paper, smoke cigarettes, and drink their coffee as the kids watched Saturday morning cartoons. Dad pulled the newspaper moderately away from his face; Tina's eyes wandered up towards dad's, both smirking. Still playing it cool, even though the excitement on the inside of my body was bouncing around like a kid with severe ADHD (Attention-deficit/hyperactivity disorder), I sipped my coffee, never moving my head; only my eyes wandered back and forth between each one of them.

"What do you want now?" dad asked dryly. "Well, there is this new teen dance club that opened up. Patty and the girls want me to go tonight. They want to pick me up at 6 p.m. May I please go?" He knew I wanted to go. I never used the polite words, "May I," unless I wanted something or wanted to go do something.

Sipping the coffee, became slurping the coffee as my eyes rolled back and forth to two smirking, eye-locking adults torturing me with an answer.

"What do you think?" dad questioned. Tina. My mouth gaped. What does he mean? What does she think? Who in the Sam hell is she? I thought to myself.

Tina reached next to her chair on the floor, grabbed her purse, and pulled out twenty dollars, handing it to me. "I say let her go get her dance on," she winked. The 5'8 woman, with dark curly hair, blue eyes, and a little on the chubby side, surprised me with her friendly gesture. Nah, I was just kidding. She was trying to play, get on Lindsey's right side. Too bad it would not happen. Putting on a fake smile, I thanked them both, placed my coffee cup in the sink, and made a dash for my bedroom, opening my closet door, trying to contemplate on what outfit I wanted to wear that night. A girl must look good while getting her dance on, you know? Spending all day intoxicated by this new night club for teens, I could hardly remain calm! Becoming more anxious when it was time to get ready, I could have almost crawled out of my skin.

I took a shower enthusiastically, dressed in a jean mini skirt came up a little shorter than the mid-thigh, a red blouse, and red flats. Blowing my long hair dry, I spiral curled it and then applied my makeup slightly darker than usual. A mauve lipstick added the finishing touches to my soft pink lips, along with some lavender perfume. Giving myself one last look over in my vanity mirror, I heard a knock on the front door. It was time to hit the club and shred the dance floor with the girls.

Arriving at the club, we paid our door fee and entered. It wasn't quite what I had expected at first. There was a square wood dance floor with a stage behind it. It was dark, with colorful lights that messed with your eyes until they adjusted to it.

A good-looking DJ in the DJ booth reverberating music, with just a few teens standing on and around the dance floor. Figuring that it was still early, and we were one of the first few to arrive, I might give it some time before I blew the joint. The DJ peered over at us and stepped down from the booth, strolling right towards us. Extending his hand out, shaking each one of ours, he introduced himself as David, the club owner. David also handed us a tape of his, letting us know he was a musician. He allowed young, up-and-coming musicians to come into his club on certain nights and perform to an audience on the stage behind the dance floor. I thought it was cool.

Immediately, I developed a crush on David and couldn't wait to get home and listen to his tape.

The club was named "Sweet Sixteen" and became our new home on the weekends. David even started having a camera crew from a local television station on Saturday nights to record everyone dancing. We could watch it on the local station on Sunday mornings. The family would get up and watch. Dad would video record it, and we all had some great laughs watching us dance, and they loved to poke fun at me.

Hcy, at least we were laughing.

Dad made us laugh and have fun with us when he wanted to. He would take us to work with him at the barracks. We would go on seven-mile hikes with the troops, play in the recreation rooms. He would make his troops buy things we were selling from the schools to win the biggest prizes. The Army also had a family fun day. We played games, ate tons of great food, and even got to ride in and drive the Bradley tanks. He loved to show off his family outside the home, but put the fear of death inside the house. Even when he was making you laugh and having fun with you, you still knew he was a monster. He was like Jekyll and Hyde. You just never knew when Jekyll would appear, so you always had your guard up.

Chapter Eight
99 Bottles Of Beer On The Wall

Announcing he was marrying Tina in November 1990, I knew that shit was coming. The terrible thing was, he was still sneaking down to Katie's apartment and hadn't told her yet. He was about to shred that poor, sweet woman's heart to miniature pieces, and he didn't give a damn. But I am glad she would no longer be with him. She deserved better.

Standing at the courthouse as the two heaps of shit got married, I yawned, rolled my eyes, and thought about how I had better things to do, like jumping off a cliff.

Becoming an alcoholic, I drank a lot of a party heavily when I wasn't out dancing at the teen club. With the holidays approaching, I started drinking even more when I noticed dad wasn't doing much about purchasing anything for the kids for Christmas or getting a lovely tree. Giving her props for stepping in, Tina bought presents and a Christmas tree, baked cookies with the kids, and helped me make it festive for them. Dad ended up helping a little.

As my life was spiraling out of control, I noticed dad wasn't right. The hair stood up on the back of your neck when he was in your presence. Looking into his eyes, there wasn't anything there. There was just coldness. It sent chills up your spine.

Walking into the kitchen one night, I accidentally stumbled upon him, pulling out a bottle of alcohol hidden from behind the fridge. He put his pointer finger to his lips. "Shhh, don't tell Tina," he whispered.

"I won't," I whispered back. It seems like I wasn't the only closet drinking in the home. With him, it scared me. Psycho and alcohol don't mix! I was tired of keeping all his secrets, but I did. He was just one big cosmic lie.

Tina was busy making lunch for the younger kids; baby Jason, nine months old, awoke from his nap and was crying. He shared the master bedroom with Dad and Tina since there wasn't any more room in the boy's room. After Tina moved in, my poor brother Jake was stuck sharing a small bedroom with two-year-old Zach.

Having her hands full, I told Tina I would get the baby for her. Approaching the crib, I picked up Jason, gave him a little kiss on his cheek, then squinted my eyes, not believing what I saw. There was a black and blue handprint across baby Jason's face! Standing still for a moment, I smoothed my fingers along with the handprint as I got a lump in my throat, and my stomach was in knots.

This time, fear didn't take over me. It was anger! How could my dad be such a cowardly bastard from hell and hit a baby? Oh, wait. He started beating me when I was an infant. What was I thinking?

Carrying the baby into the kitchen, I made Tina aware of the handprint shaped bruise across

Jason's face. "Oh, I saw it. Your dad said he hit his face against the bars in the crib." She then continued to cook.

"And you believe that?" I questioned with annoyance.

"Oh, Lindsey. Your dad wouldn't do something like that." she furrowed her brows and threw up her chin.

Walking towards the highchair, I placed the baby in it, strapped him in, and then put the tray over it, giving him a few little cheerios while waiting on his lunch.

Striding into the living room, I sat down on the couch and turned dad's stereo on.

Turning on one of my dad's very albums and flipping it to one of our favorite songs, I lay back on the couch and stared at the textured ceiling on the wall, listening to the lyrics. I've swallowed my pride for you...

I've lived and lied for you...

I make you laugh...

You make me cry...

I believe it's time for me to fly...

I'm tired of lying for him that was for sure. Staring at the textured ceilings and losing myself in my thoughts, something popped into my head that I recalled happening that I found to be weird. When we first came back to Georgia, my dad took us through the drive-thru at McDonald's. He pulled to the side to help my sister and brother get situated with their Happy Meals. A police officer pulled up along the side of us. He got out of his car and asked for my dad's license. He then gave my dad a dirty look and wasn't very nice to him at all. He wanted to know if we were okay, then told my dad he needed to move along. He didn't want dad there. It made me wonder if my dad had broken the law or something while we were away? Had he done something we didn't know about? Maybe I was overthinking? I was indeed about to find out, and my life was about to change forever.

Chapter Nine

The Night My Life Changed Forever

It was February 1991, and I was in a deep slumber in my room. The sound of my bedroom door creaking open awoke me, but I kept my eyes shut, thinking it was just dad or Tina checking on us before they went to bed. But then, I felt someone standing over me and feeling them breathe, hearing them breathe. Then the tight grip of a man's hand shook my arm, and he spoke. "Lindsey, get up and come into the kitchen quietly," dad whispered.

Opening my eyes, I glanced up to see my dad's face damn near in mine with the powerful smell of liquor on his breath. It was in the middle of the night, and I wondered why my dad wanted me to get up and come to the kitchen. With him, you didn't ask questions; you just followed his orders, so I did. Rubbing my somnolent eyes, my feet hurried down the hallway and into the kitchen. My eyes squinted at the intense light of the kitchen, and I struggled to gain focus to adjust my eyes. My eyes gazed down at the old round kitchen table, where there were two small glasses of whiskey with ice melting in them.

"Sit down and drink," dad demanded.

"What?" I was confused.

"You heard me. Sit down and drink that glass of whiskey," dad pointed.

"I don't want to," I replied in a shaky voice. "You will do what I say," dad gritted his teeth, becoming angry.

My legs felt like Jell-O as I slowly strode over to the chair, sat down, and took small sips of the watered-down whiskey that still burned at my throat as it proceeded down. "Finish it," he demanded again.

"I am," I replied, fighting some tears. I didn't know why my dad was doing this or what would happen next, imagining another beating coming my way. God, please don't beat me, was all I kept thinking.

"I'll be right back." He left the kitchen and strolled down the hallway quietly.

When dad returned, he held in his hands a black nightie, black garter belt, and black stockings.

"Go put these on," he said, as he handed them to me. I took them and did what he told me to do.

Confused, I hadn't a clue what was going on.

Slowly, I put one foot in front of the other and walked out of the bathroom. When I turned my head and peered into the living room, dad was sitting on the couch with his shorts pulled down, fully exposing himself to me.

"Come here," he demanded yet again.

As I slowly strode towards him, my legs felt like noodles; my heart pounded against my chest, my body shuddered, hot tears streamed down my cheeks; I got tunnel vision and thought for a moment I was going to collapse from fear. I could barely hold my head up. Glancing over at the deadbolt on the front door, I knew if I tried to make a run for it, dad would catch me before I could get away. If I screamed for Tina, he would probably kill us all. It was for the best that I just did what he told me to do. Obey his every command. I was getting ready to be treated like his cheap whore, not his daughter. Standing in front of him, he pulled me close, putting his sleazy hands all over my fourteen-year-old body. He went down on me. Closing my eyes, I thought of something else to take my mind off what the scumbag was doing to me. He then sat up and forced me between his legs and made me go down on him, smacking me in the back of the head if I didn't have my mouth wrapped around his penis the way he wanted. While this was going on, my sister stumbled into the living room. Dad jumped up, pulled up his shorts, and put her back to bed. When he returned, he told me to go to the bathroom and put my pajamas back on.

Quickly, I ran to the bathroom and changed. I couldn't get out of that sleazy nightie fast enough. I felt so filthy, so dirty, so humiliated. Grabbing a razor from the bathroom cabinet, I started dragging it across my wrists. I wanted to die. Dad came into the bathroom, took the razor from me; as I was crying so hard, I could barely catch my breath, and told me to take my cry baby ass back to bed. If I had a gun, I would have put it to his head and pulled the friggin' trigger.

I went to bed, lying there in a fetal position, shaking, silently crying, gasping, and trying to take in everything that just took place. That night, Dad robbed me. I was depleted of everything. I would never be myself again. I would trust no one again. I would never be the same person I once was. Lindsey was gone. I wondered what my mom and family would think if I told them what happened to me. Would they believe me? Would anyone believe me? That night, I went numb. That night changed me forever. The sad thing, he wasn't done with me yet.

Chapter Ten

My Childhood Was Stolen

Rays of sunlight glowed through the dark brown sheet that was still hanging like a curtain on my bedroom window. Squinting my weary eyes, glancing over towards my sister's bed, I could see that she was gone. "Damn! I am late for school," I mumbled to myself, leaping out of bed. My body felt weak, and I ached between my legs. The taste of stale whiskey still lingered on my breath from the night before. I peered out the window. Dad's car was still in the parking lot, but Tina's was gone, which meant he allowed me to sleep in on purpose. He was probably too scared that I would go to school and tell someone about him. Being known as a troublemaker at school like anyone would ever believe me, eh? Turning on my stereo at a low volume, so he knew I wasn't awake yet, I then went and sat down on the chair in front of my vanity mirror and stared at the new Lindsey since the old one was gone. My wrists burned from the razor cuts and my head hurt from dad pulling my hair.

Wondering what I was going to do, a song on the radio caught my attention—a song by my favorite band, Aerosmith.

Honey, honey, what's your problem…

Tell me it ain't right…

Was it daddy's cradle robbin'…? That made you scream at night...

My mouth gaped, and I sat motionlessly. Leaping onto my bed, clenching my teeth together, shoving my face into the pillow, I just wanted to scream. Wanting to wash his filth from me, I grabbed some clean clothes and quietly made my way to the bathroom, locking the door behind me so the pervert wouldn't help himself and come right on in. There wasn't enough soap, and the water wasn't hot enough to get his dirty grime off me. By the time I stepped out of the shower, my skin was beet red with steam flowing from it. And I still felt dirty.

It's like an itch you can't scratch.

Getting dried off and dressed as quickly as I could, stepping out of the bathroom, there he was. To the right of me. Mr. Pervert Pedophile himself.

"Come here," he asked of me calmly. Slowly, I approached him. He pulled me close to him, hugging me. "I'm sorry for what I did last night. Call it molestation or whatever you want, but I thought about it. If grandma and grandpa would ever have done anything like that to me, I can't imagine."

"It's okay," I responded in a nervous voice.

"It's our little secret, okay?"

"Okay."

He then left for work.

I went back to my room and lay on my not so comfy bed. "No. No, it's not okay," I muttered. If you touch my sister or brother, I will kill you, I thought. And it just wasn't a thought; it was a promise. Mess with me, but don't mess with them. You will answer to God a lot sooner than you think.

At dinner that night, I ate little. Just a couple of forceful bites made me gag when I swallowed— picked at my dinner with my fork until I finally gave in and excused myself from the table. The kids were all laughing and smiling while eating. They all appeared so innocent, so sweet. How could anyone steal a child's innocence or even hurt them? A child should never fear their parent in how I feared my dad. I believed he could kill if he wanted to. Hell, it was the only thing he hadn't done yet, although he did once try.

Dragging my feet down the hallway, my legs felt like concrete. My life felt like it was draining from me. I went into my room, shutting the door behind me. Kneeling by my bedroom window, I propped my elbow up on the windowsill; tears escaped my eyes, streaming down my cheeks. We weren't allowed to cry, but I didn't give a single care if he caught me crying. A beating was nothing compared to what he had done to me the night before. My sister strolled into the room; I quickly wiped my cheeks with the sleeves of my shirt.

"Why are you crying?" she softly asked.

"I'm not," trying to play it off.

"Yes, you are," she argued.

"Go to bed," I replied with annoyance. So she did, pouting.

I got off my knees, turned the stereo on low, turned off the light, and climbed into that springy piece of crap bed. I rolled to my side, pulled my knees to my chest, and thought, this is no more extended home.

Chapter Eleven

The Night He Stole My Innocence

Leaning against the bike racks behind the high school, watching a sea of teenagers with their arms full of books and backpacks, laughing, most probably coming from good homes with great parents, I lit a cigarette and took a couple of puffs, wishing it were myself laughing too. I mean, I laughed, but it was faked or forced; I was feeling numb deep inside.

Waiting for the girls to arrive, I was at school but wasn't planning on staying there. Skipping school so much, hell, I didn't even know where any of my classes were and probably had cobwebs growing in my locker.

Lighting another cigarette, taking two puffs, the girls came shuffling towards me. Telling them my plan, we huddled for a moment, trying to decide what house we were going to for the school day. We ended up choosing Patty's since her parents were gone all day, and our chances of being caught by her parents were slim.

Dashing across the parking lot of the high school, we made it to the main road. It had been raining that morning; we took our shoes off and splashed through the cold puddles of water on the side of the road, all the way to Patty's.

Snacking, drinking sodas, painting our nails, laughing, and joking was how we spent our day until it was time to go home when school let out. I had to time it just right, or dad and Tina would become suspicious and check and see if I was at school that day.

Making it home in time, dad wanted me to hurry along and get my room packed quickly. He had bought a house in our old neighborhood. It was down the street by the creek. It didn't take us long to move everything out of the apartment. There wasn't much to carry out. Since dad promised he wouldn't touch me again, I took one last look at the apartment before we left. I was saying goodbye to the terrible memories that had happened in there and hoping to make good ones in our new home.

Arriving at our new home, dad and Tina rushed to get things unloaded so they could get the U-Haul back the next morning. Dad was cheap like that. We were exhausted by the time we were done unpacking. Dad ordered pizza for dinner. We devoured in minutes from hunger. Dad gave me my own room. The situation did not set right with me. He had never given me my room. It meant he could come in anytime he pleased. He had complete access to me. I was so scared. The feeling in the pit of my stomach reminded me that dad always broke promises.

Later that night, I awoke to the sound of my bedroom door creaking open. My light turned on with the sound of footsteps shuffling towards me. Dad hovered over me. I could hear him breathe. I could feel their eyes gazing over me.

"Wake up," dad shook my arm. I didn't budge, pretending I was still asleep.

"Wake up," he shook my arm again. Squinting my eyes open against the bright light, dad climbed on top of me, pulling my blue nightgown with flowered print up, and started tugging my panties down. "Stop, daddy," I pleaded. The tears hot tears flowed down my hazy eyes, my body trembled, I wanted to scream, but I had no voice, and I was now experiencing terror as he placed a pillow over my face, raping and suffocating me.

Locking my knees together, he just kept beating them with his fists apart. Dad became angrier. Not being able to fight him off because he was so much stronger, I gave in. The only way I could gain any access to air was by turning my head to the side forcefully, finding a small crack where the air was flowing in. It wasn't enough, still gasping and straining to breathe, but at least it was helping somewhat.

When he was through with me, he pulled the pillow away from my face. I gasped. My lungs were starving for air. Looking down, still crying, wheezing, and coughing, he was observing some bloodstains on my blue-flowered nightgown.

He threw me a smile as he pulled my panties up. "You were still a virgin. Good girl."

Sick fuck.

If I had a shotgun, I would have blown his head off. What a filthy rapist, child molesting bastard, I thought, pulling my nightgown down and my blankets tightly over me. Dad placed a twenty-dollar bill on top of my dresser. "This is for the teen club tomorrow night," he smiled. Then he strolled over, turned out the light, and shut my bedroom door.

I lay there, crying silently. The tears damn near soaked my pillowcase. Why was this happening to me? I knew I was always in trouble and did wrong, but did I deserve this? Was this my fault? Was it the way I dressed? Was it because he still loved my mom, and I looked like her?

I never thought about death until that night or suicide. I wanted to die. I wanted it to all be over with. But first, I wanted my sister and brother to be safe, back home in Indiana with mom. If I committed suicide now, then who would be his next target? For now, I would remain to be his target to keep the other kids safe. He could hit me, beat me, molest me, rape me, just as long as it was me and not the other kids.

Peering over at the twenty-dollar bill on the dresser, I knew it was "hush money." I cried so hard I couldn't catch my breath, feeling so filthy, dirty, and like a paid whore. Rolling over onto my side, staring at the blank white wall in front of me, my eyes burned from all the tears I cried that night. For the first time, I just wanted my mom. This place no longer felt like home. It never did since the day we arrived to live with dad.

Chapter Twelve
Feeling Numb

Rays of sunlight shone through the cracks of the dark brown sheet hanging over my bedroom window. Dad had failed to get a curtain for my room, and by then, I didn't care. I had worse things to worry about, like how the hell to keep him out of my room and his hands off me. I woke up a different person on that February day. My life changed forever. It would never be the same. My brain was shutting down, and I felt like I was running on autopilot. I didn't care about life anymore.

As I sat up, my head hurt. I ached between my legs. My thighs hurt, with bruises on them, where he had pounded his fists against them to get my legs to spread open. I gazed at the blood on my nightgown, my stomach became nauseous. Those words he spoke spiraled around in my head. "You were a virgin. Good girl." I damn near needed my trashcan. My mouth watered as I fought back the vomit.

Wanting to wash his filth away, I grabbed some clean clothes, strolled to the bathroom, passed dad, Tina, and the kids, laughing and having breakfast at the kitchen table. Dad peered at me and smiled. I didn't return one, just walked into the bathroom, shutting and locking the door.

Scrubbing my skin in steaming hot water, I didn't know that I was washing away evidence. Sitting in that tub was a huge mistake.

I didn't know any better.

I told daddy's little secrets, who would believe me now? When I was done with my bath and getting dressed, I threw my nightgown in the laundry hamper, mistake number two. Dammit, if I only knew.

The girls and I spent the early afternoon at the mall to kill some time before hitting the club that night. Dad gave me his ATM card and told me I could take fifty dollars out to spend. More "hush money" was all it was. But I took it and treated the girls to lunch in the food court.

After filling their tummies, the girls searched for cute boys; I searched for something to purchase with the rest of the fifty dollars dad had given me.

Passing by a store window, something caught my eye. Smiling, I went into the store and picked out a diary, buying it. Now, I had something that I could share all of my secrets, feelings, and thoughts.

And it had a lock and key. I couldn't wait to get home and write in it!

Later that night at the teen dance club, I had an odd feeling overcome me and a knot in the pit of my tummy as we were leaving. Stepping back away from the sea of teenagers flowing out the exit door, I looked around. It was as if it would be the last time I ever saw the home away from the horror house again. Searching the room with my eyes, they locked with David's, and he threw me a pearly white smile that made my heart flutter. Of course, I had a crush on him even though he was twenty-five, and I was fourteen. Who could pass up tall, blonde, blue eyes and a talented singing voice?

Walking out of the exit, I shook the feeling off as being paranoid. Dashing to catch up with the girls, I got into the back seat of the car and closed the door. As we pulled away, I looked back at the flashing pink neon sign that read, "Sweet Sixteen." Blinking my eyes to fight my tears, I was kidding myself. I had a gut feeling I would never be back.

Chapter Thirteen
I'm Telling Daddy's Secret

Every morning I would wake up feeling so worthless, drained, empty, ashamed, numb, and petrified of what dad might do to one of us kids that day. A beating? Or would he sneak into my room to touch me or rape me again? You never knew what was going to happen in the house of horror living with that monster.

Spending most of my days in my room when I didn't have school or after school, I would lie in my bed and write in my diary. Keeping track of times, days, the things he did to me and the kids, and how I wanted to die. I no longer was a kid that had dreams and hope. He stole that from me. Now, I was a kid fighting to survive a parent that was hurting me when he was supposed to be protecting me. No matter how many baths or showers I took, I always felt dirty because of him.

Writing in my diary one afternoon, hungry, I made my way to the kitchen and made a turkey and cheese sandwich loaded with mustard. As I sat at the kitchen table, I glimpsed dad strolling into the bathroom. Seconds later, he walked back out, holding a cup. No toilet flushed, no running water; I found it quite odd.

Continuing to eat my sandwich, dad strolled into the bathroom, holding his cup again. He shut the door behind him. Seconds later, he wandered back out. We locked eyes as he passed by me. My chewing became slower; then nausea hit the pit of my stomach. I spit the small portion of the chewed-up sandwich onto my plate. My body trembled, my heart palpitated, my vision tunneled as the room spun, and my breathing became labored. Dad had liquor hid in the bathroom; I just knew it. The worse thing about it, I knew what was coming next. He would be in my room on top of me, raping me later that night.

Fighting back the tears, remaining calm, I waited until he left the living room so that I could talk to Tina. There was no way I could handle any more abuse from dad. The thought of him raping me or touching me again made me want to put a gun to his head and pull the trigger.

Dad left the room, so I dashed over to Tina. "Tina, I have to talk to you in private," my voice shook.

"What's wrong, Lindsey?" she was concerned.

"Shhh, he will hear you," I whispered. Dad entered the room, so I played it cool. "Tina, can you run me over to Courtney's picking up my sweater?" I was hoping she would get the hint.

"Sure. Let me get my shoes and purse." Thank God, she got the hint. Getting into the car, as we pulled out of the driveway, I covered my face with my hands, spilling out tears, screaming outcries that shocked the hell out of Tina.

She pulled over to the nearest gas station, freaking out, with a concerned look on her face. "What's the matter, Lindsey?" she cried out. "Dad's been molesting me, and he raped me," I screamed and cried.

"Oh my God," she cried, too. "I just want someone to believe me. Someone to help me, "I pleaded. Dad might kill me now that I told his secret," I bellowed out.

"I believe you. He was a week late getting you kids because there was an investigation for possibly molesting my three-year-old niece. She said that he put his private part in her mouth. Oh my God, she wasn't lying. They dismissed it, as she must have heard it from a playground or TV," she told me with a terrified look.

Tina and I cried for a few minutes and then drove to Courtney's, using her phone to call the police. On the way there, I had so many mixed emotions going on; I was an emotional mess. All I wanted was to come home to Georgia to live with my dad, someone I looked up to no matter how many beatings he gave us, someone I loved and adored, and he betrayed me in the worst way he could. Because of him, I would never be normal again.

At Courtney's, I had to tell the police everything, detail by detail. My body trembled, and I could feel my face flush with everyone crowded around, listening to me. I told them about the blood and semen on my pajamas and my diary under my springy ass bed mattress. Tina left in a hurry, so dad would suspect that anything was going on.

The police loaded me into the squad car's back, and we headed over to dad's. There were police everywhere when we pulled up, and the neighbors were, of course, being nosey. They ordered dad to stand outside on the porch while they searched the house and my room. An officer came out to tell me she couldn't find my pajamas or diary. "That's because Tina heard where I put them. That's why she left in a hurry," I responded angrily. The police officer said she would talk with her, but Tina was not giving in. What a freaking bitch.

My brother and sister were clueless about why they were in a police car. I reassured them not to worry; dad did something wrong. I didn't want to tell them the truth. They were too young to understand.

Chapter Fourteen
Protective Custody, Foster Homes, And Regrets

Social workers placed my sister and me into protective custody in one home, my brother in another. I threw a fit, wanting us all to stay together. It turns out the state doesn't care what you want. Regrets of telling on dad were already filling my mind. But then again, he should be punished for what he had done, especially to that little three-year-old. I was even more disgusted to find that out.

A caseworker drove us to a trailer park, pulling up in front of a trailer, and an elderly lady was there to greet us. With only the clothes on our back, we followed her inside. It was late, so we went straight to bed. Our bed was in the living room. It was dark, so we didn't get to get a good look around. Jessica fidgeted for a while, then fell asleep.

Tossing and turning, I couldn't take my mind off all the horrible matters that had taken place since we returned to Georgia. I wondered if mom had been notified of the incident yet. What did she think about all that had happened? Did she believe me? I felt I had to stay brave for my sister and brother's sake; the truth was I was fucking scared out of my mind. What was going to happen to us next? Tina's face flashed in my mind, and oh, how I wanted to choke her for the missing pajamas and diary. I was furious about that situation. How could you protect a pedophile and child rapist? To me, she was just as sickening as he was.

For the next three days, my sister and I stayed in bed in the living room, only getting up to shower, eat, and go to the bathroom. The older woman had some other foster kids there, and she wasn't very nice. I kept my sister close to me, never letting her out of my sight.

After the third day of protective custody, the social worker separated us again. This time, my sister and brother temporarily went to a foster home until my mom came to pick them up. I had to go to a different home to stay behind to testify against my dad in court. It was heartbreaking. I didn't even get to say goodbye to my siblings, and I made the caseworker promise me she would let me know when they were back home in Indiana safe with mom. The caseworker did. It relieved me. Now, I just had to worry about myself.

Pulling up to the foster home that I would live at while going through the court battle to put dad in prison, or at least try to, my stomach was in knots, once again frightened, not knowing who these people were or how they would treat me. God, I just wanted it to be over. I just wanted my mom.

The house was a two-story, well kept on the outside, painted white, nothing fancy. The caseworker and I stepped out of the car, still with just the clothes on my back, feeling rather disgusting, because you would have thought someone would have gone to dad's and got me some clothes by now; we walked up to the door, she knocked, and a short, stocky lady with short salt and pepper hair answered smiling.

The caseworker introduced us, then she quickly left, leaving me alone and afraid. Deborah, my foster mom, hollered up a flight of stairs. Still standing motionless in the same place, greeted at the door, my eyes searched the home. The living room peered to be warm and inviting, with grey plush furniture, a huge T.V., and cute little country style knickknacks set out on the end tables and in a lit curio cabinet. There was light beige clean carpet running through the home, except in the kitchen, where there was clean beige ceramic tile to match the rug.

Deborah stood at the foot of the staircase and hollered out for a group of girls once again. My knees almost buckled underneath me when I saw four girls trampling down the stairs. My mouth gaped as I knew them all from school. For a split second, I wish I didn't exist. The girls introduced themselves cheerfully. I had only seen them at school; I didn't know them. Having no clue that I saw these girls around, and they had possible horrific homes, lives too, made me feel like I was not alone.

Stacy, who had long deep brown hair, brown eyes, a chubby face, with a medium build, grabbed me by the arm, dragging me up the stairs eagerly to show me my new room. The girls observed me as I peered around in silence. There were two bunk beds, a stereo, clothing, and shoes all over the place, like the dressers and fucking closet exploded.

"I'm Maggie." A tall girl with blonde hair that was just past the shoulder, blue eyes, tanned, and a bright white smile introduced herself. I returned the introduction.

"Lindsey, you can put your belongings in this dresser and your clothes in the closet. The hangers are over there," she pointed.

Shrugging my shoulders, peering down at the beige carpet, well, what you could see of it because of the explosion of clothing, "I don't have any clothes yet. Nobody has even bothered to get them from my dad's house. Been wearing the same damned clothing for over three days now," I sighed with embarrassment.

"Oh girl, we got you," a girl named Michelle called out. She was short, shoulder-length brown hair, brown eyes, and a slender build. The girls got together and scurried around the room. Maggie, another fostered teen, found an unopened package of panties; It relieved me to see that they fit! The other girls explored the room and placed all the clothing that would fit me into a folded-up pile. "It's almost dinner and bedtime. Here are some pajama pants and a t-shirt to match. The bathroom is downstairs to your left. Go take a hot bath and put these on," Michelle smiled.

Going down the line, I gave each one of them a hug. "You don't know how much I appreciate this." I fought back some tears. I was so enthusiastic. A hot bath and clean clothing, a warm dinner was heaven after all I had been through the last week. Dinner was terrific, and I complimented my foster parents for it. Fried chicken, mashed potatoes, and green beans, then a bowl of ice cream for dessert. My tummy was ready to pop.

My foster parents were fostering a new baby too, and I felt sorry for him. Desperately, I wanted to ask why he was taken from his home and parents, but I knew it was none of my business.

Bedtime approached, and Stacy allowed me to have the top bunk bed, which I was delighted. Lights went out, and it felt incredible that there were no springs from the mattress stabbing me all over my body. The bed was soft heavenly! Each of us girls told our stories of why we were in the foster home to begin. They were all there from some abusive families, just like me. Suddenly, I didn't feel so alone, but I was frightened about what would happen next. It petrified me to tell them my story, but I did.

There was no judgment. The girls made sure that

I needed to hear the words I had not yet heard. "It's not your fault. You did nothing wrong, dad did. Don't be ashamed. He would be the one that should be ashamed for what he did. And never be ashamed to tell your story." Thank God the room was dark. As they spoke, tears soaked my pillow.

I lay there quietly that night; thoughts of what happened were on instant replay in my mind. Then I thought about my friends. My eyes popped open, and I furrowed my brows when I thought back to an incident with Patty.

When we were living in the apartment, we had a sleepover one night. My sister, Jessica, had to sleep in my brother's room so Patty could sleep in my room in my sister's bed. Waking in the middle of the night, glancing over at my sister's bed, it was empty. Patty was not in bed. She had always commented on how "hot" my dad was, and she was very promiscuous; she slept with every guy that crossed her path. Patty was repeatedly in fights with other girls because of it. Patty had always been a bit of a mystery to us; we never knew how old she really was or what grade she was really in. You could never get a truthful answer out of her. We just blew it off and let it go because she was a friend. Never did I get up that night. She stayed at the apartment. I didn't want to discover anything I didn't want to find out or see. So, I just kept it to myself.

I figured it was consensual, and it was just best that I told no one. I pushed it to the back of my mind until now. I am about 99 percent sure Patty slept with my dad that night, and damn, the thought disgusted me. Pushing all the evil thoughts out of my head, squeezing my eyes tightly, I finally fell into a peaceful, deep slumber—the best part of falling asleep that night. I didn't have to worry about the bedroom door creaking open and dad hovering over me.

Chapter Fifteen
Finally, Going To Court

Somehow, it had got around the entire school that my dad raped and molested me. Not that I stayed at school anyway and always hung out at one of the girl's homes for the school day, or we just ended up hanging at the bike racks, it still bothered me I was getting stares, kids were mumbling to each other as they walked by hell, even some of them giggled. I guess getting raped and molested is funny? Leaving the bathroom, I ran into Maggie, stopping to chat with her briefly before heading to the bike racks. I didn't want her to know

I was skipping school. A voice behind me said, 'That's the girl that was being "fucked" by her father," she then giggled. My purse flew in one direction as I flew in another, charging at her like a raging bull! A group of girls, including Maggie, broke up the fight. Maggie told me the girl wasn't worth it; she handed me my purse as I cried and walked away. The girl's friends shook their heads in disbelief over what their friend had said to me. Maggie strolled down one hallway; I strolled out the exit door, crying and lighting up a cigarette, heading to the bike racks. I was getting a "screw everyone and everything" frame of mind. I approached the bike rack; my friends were all worried cause they had heard of what happened to me. They wanted to know if I was okay. "I'm going to be just fine," I lied. Then lit another cigarette, coughed twice, then forged a beaming smile.

It was pleasant living in a home full of girls my age. We all got along well except for me and the foster parent's actual daughter, Michelle. She always had her nose in the air and didn't like the attention I received from the other girls or had more friends than she did. She could get lost for all I cared. I introduced the girls to the teen club. My foster parents allowed me to go a few times, just not every weekend. We weren't allowed to do much. David had even heard about what happened to me and was happy to see me again. He gave me his address to write letters and keep in touch. We never knew if we were going to see each other as well. It seemed like it was taking forever to get a court date with dad. Nobody ever came to the foster home to talk to me about my case or the things he did. I didn't even have a children's advocate. I was becoming more depressed and feeling alone. I wasn't allowed to talk to my mom or anyone in the family. Thrown into the foster home and left in the dark. It was great.

Getting into trouble again, my foster parents caught me skipping school. Everyone brought a report card home but me. I hated to break the news to them, but I hadn't been to a single class all year and hadn't received a report card either.

The joke was on them. The foster parents took away all my privileges. Am I not your maid this week? The foster kids had the privilege of cleaning their house with a five-dollar allowance at the end of the week.

To make matters worse, my foster parents went on a diet because they were overweight, along with their daughter. Where was the fairness with this? I was fourteen years old and walking stick, barely weighing one-hundred pounds. I was going to starve to death.

Outstanding.

At Easter, they made me wear some silly dress that hung way below my knees and some sandals. Easter was at the grandparent's house. Thank God, it was in the middle of nowhere, where nobody could see me. I never saw that dress again after that day. Wonder what happened to it? Hopefully, someone burned the damned thing.

My foster mom bellowed out from downstairs that she needed me, so I trampled down the stairs to see what she wanted from me. She wanted to let me know I had a court date the next morning to testify against dad. Wow, I only got a one-day notice to prepare for this? She also scooted a box towards me. A caseworker had dropped off my shoes and clothing. I was so happy to see that! I raced upstairs with the box, ready to wear my clothes finally.

Rummaging through the box, clothing and shoes were missing. A pair of my first Nike's mom had worked her ass off to get me for Christmas was gone.

"That witch of a woman." I raised my voice in aggravation.

"What's wrong with you?" Stacy curiously asked.

"My step-mom is pure evil. First the pajamas and the diary, now she stole some of my belongings. I just want to kick her ass right now."

The following morning, I got myself ready for court. After showering and fixing my hair, I put on a skin-tight red dress that stopped at the mid-thigh and red flats. I wasn't thinking clearly. It wasn't the sort of clothing you should wear into court for a rape and molestation case, but then again, daddy shouldn't be touching his daughter under no circumstances.

As I was sitting in the courthouse, my stomach turned as if I were going to vomit. Thank God I didn't eat any breakfast that morning. My nerves wouldn't allow me to eat. A tall skinny white male, dressed in a suit and tie, holding a briefcase, strode over and sat next to me on the bench. The room was spinning, and I didn't hear a word he had spoken, just nodding my head, pretty sure my brain had shut down from fear. It was overwhelming, and all too much. After what seemed like hours, but only minutes, they finally called us into the courtroom. It was tiny. It was damn near the size of a master bedroom closet, maybe a tad bigger. As I stood swaying nervously in front of the judge, it was so quiet you could hear a pin drop. I look to my left. They finally ushered my dad in, wearing handcuffs, in his full military uniform, behind his back. What, did they pick him up from work, temporarily arrest him, then plan on dropping him back off later? What a joke.

The judge swore us in. He then asked me to tell him my story. My body felt as if it were going to shut down. I wasn't sure what words I could use. Nobody had discussed anything with me, so I swayed my body back and forth with a nervous disposition and started from the first night the asshole came into my room. Drowning in humiliation, it relieved me to finish the last words of what had happened to me. Then I turned to my dad and whispered, "I hate you." The judge, both attorneys, glanced back and forth, trying to catch what was spoken.

The judge and lawyers chatted. I hadn't a clue what they were saying, and then my lawyer and I stepped out of the courtroom. My lawyer talked with my foster mom, and we left the courthouse. There was not another word spoken. Again, I was left in the dark. I believe they let him out on bail that morning, and I lost all faith in the justice system. He was free to do what he wanted.

And I was trapped in hell. I learned that day that children have no voice.

Chapter Sixteen

I Was Not Okay

Weeks went by; nothing. Not a single soul had contacted me any further about the case. I was trapped in the foster care system: no counseling, no victim advocate, nothing. Not being able to talk to my family for months was ripping me to shreds, as well.

Covertly, I went to the phone and called Patty one afternoon. Planning on running away, I just couldn't take living in the foster care system anymore. Depression, anger, instability, and anxiety were taking a toll on me mentally. I had to get away, feeling as if I was suffocating. Patty wanted to go with me.

Courtney wanted to as well. Maggie, my foster sister, was eavesdropping. She peered around the corner. "Can I go too?"

"Yes, you can," I sighed.

Patty and I planned to meet up at Courtney's house the following morning. We had no money and no idea of a destination. It would not be easy, but I was sure we would figure something out. At least I had hoped so!

The next morning, I threw on my skin-tight red dress and flats, the one I wore to court, fixed my hair, and acted as if I were leaving for school with Maggie by my side. We went quickly and earlier than the other girls to get a head start, since we were taking off in a different direction than the school. Maggie and I left with nothing but the clothes on our back. Bad idea; however, we didn't want anyone to suspect anything. Meeting up with Patty and Courtney, we dashed the creek. By the time we arrived, we were out of breath, so we sat down on the barrier, trying to catch our breath. Once our breathing wasn't so labored, we pulled out our cigarettes and lit one up, trying to decide what to do next.

"We should call Brad. He will know what to do," Patty suggested, taking a puff of her cigarette.

"Good idea," I responded.

We got up from the barrier and walked to the nearest gas station to call Brad. Fifteen minutes later, he came by the gas station and picked us up in his truck.

Brad said we could stay with him, his sister, and her boyfriend, who was living in the basement of Brad's mom's house. She was a sheriff that worked nights. He knew what happened to me and wanted to help. He told his sister, and she wanted to help too. His mom worked nights, so we had to hide out during the day and come out at night. At least I wasn't stuck at that crappy foster home. When we arrived, Brad introduced me to his sister Mary and Scott, her boyfriend.

Mary locked eyes with me. "Do you know why I want to help you so much?" she questioned me with a harsh voice. "Why?" I wondered.

"Because it happened to me," she smiled. Never call yourself a victim. You're a damn survivor. Got it?"

I smiled, and a tear tried to escape my eye, but I didn't allow it. What in the hell is wrong with this world? Another person just like me?

Knowing if I didn't stick around and was the crucial witness to dad's crimes, he could be released and all charges dropped against him. My mind was not reasoning, and I was so confused about what was going on at all. Nobody was helping me heal. I was lost. I was just surviving. I was trying to live again, and I didn't know how to. Running away seemed like my only escape back to reality.

Chapter Seventeen
Sweet Home Alabama

Scott and Mary thought it would be best to hide us girls outside of the state for a couple of days. Alabama was a hotel outside of state lines. Scott pawned the title to his car to get the hotel's money and help pay to feed us. They were such amazing, caring people.

Once we arrived at the hotel, we cut and dyed our hair. I had to cut my long, dish blonde hair off to my shoulders and die it black. Tears formed in my eyes as my hair hit the hotel room floor. I loved my hair. Scott and Mary left us with food, drinks, and clean clothing. Mary was a size larger than I was, but I wasn't complaining. The clothes were clean, and I had tennis shoes on my feet instead of flats. The two-headed back to Georgia for the weekend, leaving us at the hotel, making sure we made no phone calls to anyone, or let ourselves bed noticed by anyone. We made a promise not to. They would have gone to jail for assisting minor runaways. Brad wanted to stay behind, so he did.

The sunset and I grabbed a bottle of vodka hidden in a bag that I swiped from Mary and Brad's mom's liquor cabinet; of course, I didn't allow him to know that is where I had retrieved it. Telling the girls, I would be back in a few; I needed some time to myself.

Brad didn't get the hint, so he followed me out the door. There was a large hill off to the side at a hotel in the middle of nowhere where nobody could see him. I sat down on the already wet grass from the dew that was forming, but I didn't care about getting my pants wet; I had worse things going on in my fucked-up head.

The air was chilly, but not too bad since it was now nearing spring in Georgia. Mom and I had never got along, but it had been months since I could speak with her, and I missed her so much.

Brad sat down beside me, throwing his jacket around my shoulders, as my teeth chattered in between big gulps of the vodka that burned as it flowed down my throat. "You are going to drink that whole damn bottle?" he questioned.

"Hell, yes." By then, I was slurring my words, barely holding my head up.

"That's not healing or helping you. Only creating another problem," Brad said with concern, raising a brow gazing at me.

"It numbs me. It numbs the pain, the heartache, the sadness. He took everything away from me, you know?"

"You are letting him win, Lindsey. You are allowing him to destroy you."

Chucking the empty vodka bottle over the side of the hill, I then stood up; as my stomach became nauseated, I took a few steps, and before I could say a word, I was puking over the side of the hill, right into a ditch.

"C'mere." Brad held out his hand. I staggered over to him. Plopping down next to him, he allowed me to lay my head in his lap. As the earth spun from my drunken stupor, I closed my eyes; Brad ran his fingers through my hair and tucked strands behind my ears. We both fell asleep on that hill that night. The warm sunlight illuminating over the mountain the next morning woke us up. Getting up off the chilled, wet grass, we trekked back to the hotel where Scott and Mary were waiting for our arrival so we could head on back to Georgia and stay in the basement just until we could figure out our next move. Despite my head pounding from the vodka, I could function enough to make the travel back.

We were sitting in the back seat of the car; a song played on the radio as Scott was driving. Mary cranked it up. It was by Wilson Phillips. "Hold on." We all started singing together loudly. Scott shook his head, lit a cigarette, and smiled.

"This will be our song, girls. For the rest of our lives, no matter where you are, if you hear this song, think of all of us." She turned back around and continued to sing.

Every time I hear that song, I think of that moment and every one of them.

On the radio, an announcement came on about a street dance at the local Wal-Mart that evening. Everyone became enthusiastic about going to everyone except me. It was a bad idea. I expressed to everyone over and over with frustration that people and law enforcement were looking for us, and that would be one place they would most likely search. Nobody listened.

Before leaving for the street dance, Scott and Mary planned in case shit went down. I planned to stay in the basement so things wouldn't go down—my plan they didn't care too much about. As we were piling into the car, an uneasy feeling overcame me.

"Bad idea," I thought to myself as we pulled into the Wal-Mart parking lot with a sea of people and law enforcement. "Bad idea."

Stepping out of the car, we approached the crowd, and it only took less than five minutes for Courtney's older sister to spot her, pointing her out to a police officer. He ran after her. The rest of us ran in the opposite direction. Patty and I slipped underneath a truck, watching police officers run back and forth, searching past us. The coast was clear, so Patty and I hurried from underneath the car. "Oh, shit," I snapped. "Patty, turn the other way and be still," I demanded.

Thank God that the short black hair hid my identity well. Tina, the idiot–walked by, searching right past Patty and me.

Patty and I lie low, running, and hiding in one of the Port-O-Pots.

Through a hole, I peered as I watched Courtney being taken away in handcuffs by an officer. My lip quivered, my eyes teared up, but I had to hold it together. Patty and I made our last escape and ran a few blocks to a park. It was in the plan, the meeting place. Scott and Mary picked us up. I was exhausted, trembling, weak, and my heart was in the pit of my stomach. Tears streamed down my cold, flushed cheeks, and my nose was running. I was losing everything now, my best friend, too.

Arriving back at the house, we dashed to the basement. Mary had me call mom. She was buying me a plane ticket and sending me back to Indiana. I wasn't allowed to leave the state, but I couldn't go back into the foster care system either. With me being a flight risk, I was afraid they would lock me up!

Patty's parents didn't care where she was. She didn't show up for days at a time, anyway. She just planned ongoing back home. Maggie called her sister and got a bus ticket to go live with her sister in Arizona. Patty called for a ride. I hugged her, and we said our goodbyes, promising to keep in touch. Scott stayed behind, while Mary dropped Maggie off at the bus station and me at the airport. The last I remember of Maggie, we were passing the bus station windows. She was reading a book, sitting in a bright yellow chair. I never knew if Maggie made it to Arizona or not. Or if her life had been better since she arrived there. Patty didn't keep in touch either, which was expected of her. I never heard from Courtney again. It was heartbreaking. I tried everything to find her with no success.

Mary walked me into the airport to make sure I got onto the plane safely. Hugging her tightly, I couldn't have thanked her enough for all that she and Scott had done for me.

I took one last look at her, smiled, and waved before I boarded the plane. Only having a small carry-on bag with two outfits Mary had given me, I clenched the little blue jean bag tight against my chest.

Leaning my head against the cold window of the plane, I thought about the day that I sat on the front porch watching the cornfields, listening to the cicadas, and eagerly waiting for dad. I should have never left that day. I should have listened to my gut. Lindsey left Indiana, but she was never coming back, at least not the same person she used to be. Nothing will ever be the same. My body felt like a limp noodle, and I was emotionally drained. I knew it would continue. I was nowhere near healing, and I felt as if I were fighting for my life.

Chapter Eighteen

Back Home Again In Indiana

The plane touched down at the Indianapolis airport. Stepping off searching for mom, she strolled right past me. I guess the hair color and cut hid my identity well.

"Mom," I yelled and waved my arms for her. She quickly turned and rushed towards me. My brother and sister followed. We gave each other hugs and kisses, a great, much-needed family moment.

When we reached the car and got in, mom drove away from the parking garage, wasting no time. She had to get down to business.

"I have to get you checked into a mental health facility, or they will extradite you to Georgia. You're a run-away, and they need you to testify against your dad," she told me firmly.

"Okay. But I don't want to go back there," I made it clear.

"That's why we need to do this. Social Services keep calling me, asking if I have heard from you yet. I have been lying and telling them 'no.'" She adjusted her rearview mirror as we approached the interstate leading us to home.

"I said okay, mom." I leaned my head against the window of the car. She was already annoying me. "Why do I have to go to a mental health facility, anyway? I did nothing wrong."

"I told you why, Lindsey." Now she was becoming annoyed with me. I glanced in the back seat at my siblings, saying nothing more about what happened. Not sure if they knew about what dad had indeed done, I didn't want their young ears to hear about it. I didn't have a clue what was happening next to me, anyway. And when I found out, I sure would not be happy.

The next morning, mom wasted no time getting me to a mental health facility. She felt terrible when she noticed the only clothing I owned, letting me know she would go shopping and buy me more.

Facility after facility, nobody would take me in because they classified me as a run-away in another state and needed to be extradited to Georgia for dad's crimes. On our last attempt, we prayed, a facility finally took me in. It was not what I thought it would be.

After filling out the paperwork, mom kissed me on the cheek and left. The doors locked behind me. A nurse had me go into a bathroom, taking what little belonged to me, and began searching my bag. Then a strip search was in session. My behavior became erratic, furious, and violent! I didn't sign up for this shit. What the hell? Wasn't I the crazy one?

They then had a psychiatrist evaluate me. And an IQ test too. Since they wanted to let my dad, do the crime and make me do time, I played like I was some maniac with no damn common sense. They became aggravated, knowing I was just an asshole. I gave a shit-eating grin and the middle finger salute to the psychiatrist as I left the small room to the living quarters where they were taking me.

The living quarters were a nurse's station on the right, a kitchen on the left, and a dining room across the kitchen. Next to the kitchen was a classroom. "I'll pass on the classroom," I muttered to myself.

Following the nurse, gripping my bag tightly to my chest, I passed teenagers along the where she was showing me my room. There was maybe six or seven, and I wondered as I passed them if they were just like me?

"This is your room," the nurse pointed. "You will share it with Stephanie. That is your bed, your closet, and your dresser. We have a group in twenty minutes, then lunch." She quickly left the room. She then peeked her head back in the door, "I forgot to tell you, the next hallway over is the boy's rooms. No girls in the boy's hallway. No boys in the girl's hallway. Got it?"

I nodded my head. She shut the door. I rolled my eyes and sat down on the edge of my bed, still gripping my bag. Hell, I didn't have enough in that bag to fill any closet or dresser. I just tossed my bag into the closet and slammed it shut.

The handle on the door pulled down, and the door creaked open. A young black girl with short hair and a slender build strolled into the room. She folded her arms, throwing me a smile.

"I'm Stephanie," she introduced herself.

"Lindsey," I replied with a forced smile.

"So, what you in here for?"

I gazed down at the ground. "Would rather not say just yet. Sorry," I whisper.

"I understand," she nodded her head. "Well, I will see you in the group in a few minutes." She left as quickly as she came. And what is this "group" shit, anyway?

When they called us over the intercom to come to the group, Stephanie came and guided me to where I needed to go as I roamed the hallway, clueless. She let out a giggle, wrapped her arm around mine, leading me into a room. There were metal folded chairs placed in a circle, "oh hell no," I thought. Seeing this before in movies, now I knew what "group" was.

A nurse came in; everyone sat down in a chair. The teens went around the circle, introducing themselves and explaining why they were there. My turn came; I gave my first name and told them that none of their God-forsaken business! What shit being confidential?

Because I wouldn't cooperate, the nurse and I exchanged some words; mine was a hell of a lot worse than hers; I then threw the folded metal chair at her. It was a big mistake. They called a code red. I ended up locked in a padded room, where there was only a bed. I was so angry, full of rage, and they wanted me to calm down before they would allow me out of that room. There were no longer tears anymore, just built up so much rage and anger.

I went to the window as the psychiatrist came to talk to me, but too afraid to go into the small room just yet. "The moron better be," I thought.

Through the shatterproof glass, "Are you going to calm yourself down, Lindsey?" she spoke in a soft tone.

Leaning my arm against the side of the window, I wanted to punch the bitch in the face, locking eyes with her. "Are you ever going to stop treating a rape and incest victim like a damn criminal?" The woman with a college degree was speechless and didn't know how I felt. Her degree was as good as wet toilet paper to me. If you haven't been through it, don't ask or tell me how I should feel.

Some survivors of rape, incest, abuse, and molestation direct themselves into positive healing. Some don't. I was one that became negative, hated everyone and everything. I no longer saw color, only black and white. Mom came on the weekends with my siblings to visit me. Once, she brought a man that she had dated. The psychiatrist thought it would be an innovative idea that I met him, seems that I didn't trust men anymore, and I was suffering from Post-Traumatic Stress Disorder. I was in the dark and had no clue that I was suffering from PTSD.

Mom came in with just the new boyfriend, who seemed pretty nice. I mean, who would walk into someone's life and stick around knowing there was so much turmoil going on in it? He was of thick muscular build, stood about 5'8, dark brown eyes, dark brown hair cut short, and a beard. He might have seemed nice, but I still did not trust him. But the visit went well.

The following weekend, mom came for a visit with my siblings. She brought me a book that she purchased for me to read. Since when the hell did, I read; Did this woman not know me? She also bought a new diary for me. Now, that made me happy. Once again, I had something I could write in; my thoughts, emotions, and what was going on in my fucked-up mind.

Running my hand over the shiny hardcover book, it read, "Ryan White: My Own Story." It caught my attention. Remembering watching the movie when I was younger, I thought I would read the book. Looking over at mom, she was happy I liked what she brought, but I knew she had something to discuss with me.

"Spill it," I said bluntly.

"Your dad had all the charges dropped against him because you were not there for court."

We locked eyes.

I shrugged my shoulders over, rubbing my hands together roughly under the table. "I knew it was going to happen, but there was no way I was staying in that hell hole any longer. They weren't even communicating with me or getting me any help."

"Well, I can tell you that Uncle Jack and Aunt Marty believe you. Not so sure about the rest of his side."

"So, now we are playing the game of–who believes me or not? Screw that. They can believe what they want. He and I know the truth. He is a child molesting, pedophile, rapist." Suddenly, I felt sick. "I don't want to talk about this anymore. I have lost a lot; now I am losing family members. All because of him. You can go now." I stood up and hugged my mom. She left.

Grabbing my books that she brought me, I went to my room and crashed onto my bed. Been in there for over a month, and all I had done was goofed around with Stephanie. No healing process had begun. I opened my Ryan White book, turning it to page one. I read that book until it was finished. Then I reread it. What an inspiration he was. Maybe since he was such a fighter, I could be a fighter, too.

Chapter Nineteen

The Story Isn't Over Yet

Dad ended up getting caught molesting more children. He even was arrested for tying Tina to a bed naked and assaulting her.

She broke free somehow and ran down the street naked, screaming for help. Dad tried to out-run the police. He was caught with child pornography. He never spent longer than three months in jail. He received a dishonorable discharge from the Army, and I later found out they gave him an eighty-five thousand-dollar check and washed their hands of him. He ended up re-married to our next-door neighbor that knew he was a pedophile. She had a young son. She thought she could "change" him. Dad got a hold of her young son, too. It was her fault. She knew better.

I wanted to take dance lessons. Excited for something for a change and channeling my violent behavior into something positive, I had a dance recital. All dolled up waiting to go on stage, and Dana showed up at my recital, wanting me to help her extradite dad to Georgia from Ohio to put him in jail for what he did to her son. Yes, the same woman that watched as we were pulled away from the child molesting bastard. "How dare you ruin a moment that I was looking forward to. You knew better." It was all I had to say to her. My eyes filled with water as I turned and strolled away, but I fought back the tears so I wouldn't screw up my makeup.

I didn't feel bad for her. Her son? Yes, I felt terrible that his mother married and moved a child molester and rapist into their home. I had too many problems of my own, and she would not be one of them. I was sixteen now. I never healed from what happened to me. Brushing it under the rug seemed like the most reasonable thing to do, not knowing it was going to catch up to me years later. Mom and I fought all the time. I now had a stepdad. She married the man she brought to the mental health facility. He was great. I didn't have to worry about him coming into my room at night. He even bought me my first car. He treated my siblings and me as if we were his own. We were lucky mom found him.

However, I partied, drank, smoked pot, ran the streets, skipped school, and sometimes didn't show up at home, causing mom to worry about where I was.

My behavior was erratic, violent, and out of control. I had no respect for anyone, not even myself. I thought about death a lot and had tried to commit suicide quite a few times, having to have my stomach pumped one of those times. I was pissed because they wouldn't let me die.

Mom tried to get me help; I would just fight with the psychiatrist. I scared them, and they didn't want me back. The road to self-destruction was right in front of me. I jumped on the path and started skipping my ass right down it! I couldn't keep a job, was always in fights, dropped out of school because they didn't want me there, and a new nightmare was about to begin. My story wasn't over yet.

Chapter Twenty
The Story Continues

As I said in the last chapter, my story wasn't over yet. It continues. I was still losing job after job because of my anger issues or because I partied too hard, the night before and didn't show up for work the next day.

Mom and I fought always; sometimes, it would get physical. I would blackout and become violent, but I always seemed to feel terrible afterward but told no one.

The only job that I ever kept was at a Go-Kart track that my best friend's grandma owned. We would work the concession stand on Friday and Saturday nights, then pile up in carloads with cute guys and go party or cruise the strips. Did I mention hot guys? Because of what happened to me, I lived wild, carefree, and on edge. After partying, I would crash wherever I was drinking. About the only time I would go home was to shower and change into clean clothes. In the short time I was home, mom and I would argue. She wanted me to grow up and having more responsibility. I could not care less.

Mom tried everything to keep me from running the streets and getting into trouble, but I was so stubborn and hardheaded that little she could do. She finally allowed me to make mistakes and learn from them on my own. Let me tell you this much. I was about to make a huge mistake and damned sure was going to learn from it.

I got a job as a dishwasher at a local restaurant, which surprised the ladies that worked there. They didn't expect to have a teenage girl washing dishes instead of waiting tables! I met a guy there that was a cook. His name was Gage. He was nerdy, but I was a sucker for nerdy guys. Gage and I started dating, but he failed to mention one thing. He had another girl pregnant, and the girl was five kinds of Looney Tunes. She stalked me and drove me crazy. Later, we became friends. I had no clue he had dumped her and wanted nothing to do with the baby, so she was giving it up for adoption. I should have left him then. Everything seemed to go okay for me. I had a job that I was keeping, a boyfriend, partied all night, and slept all day, the life of a teenager, I guess?

Gage and I were invited to a party one night by one of my best friends, Debbie, at her boyfriend, Brian's house. It appeared to be great to me. So Gage and I went. Entering the small home that wasn't in a good part of the city, Debbie introduced Gage and me to everyone and handed us a beer.

As the night went on, the drunker we became, and the beer turned into shots of liquor. Gage and I found an empty bedroom in a drunken stupor and had sexual intercourse. Brian walked in on us; of course, he had to holler out to all the party-goers what Gage and I were doing.

When we finished, we went back to the living room, sat down on the couch, grabbing another beer. I look to my right as a bedroom door opened; Debbie and Brian caught having some fun of their own. Tilting my head back, I laughed. Later, Brian and Debbie made their way back to the party, and then things became very bizarre. Brian followed me around, whispering in my ear that he wanted me, making sexual comments about my body. I figured it was time to go. He was making me uncomfortable.

To get to the bathroom of the small house, you had to trek through the master bedroom. As I left the bathroom ready to go, Brian had the bedroom door shut, blocking me from leaving the room. A sense of panic rushes through me; chills ran up my spine. "Oh, dear God, not again," was all that was running through my panic-stricken mind. We locked eyes. "If you don't screw me, I'll kick your boyfriend's butt," he said in a violent tone.

I shivered as he threw me on the bed, while tears streamed down my cheeks. Wanting to scream, I just couldn't. All I could hear was laughter in the next room from the party. Brian unbuttoned my jeans, pulled them down, along with my panties, spread my trembling legs apart, and raped me. I covered my eyes the entire time.

I pulled up my pants, ran out of the room hysterically crying, and grabbed Gage by the arm, dashing out the front door to my car. Everyone was screaming profanity at me. I squealed tires leaving the driveway. I told Gage what happened; as I dropped him off at his home, he went in and went straight to bed! What a piece of shit. I saved him from being beaten by guys ten times bigger than him. He didn't even care.

Driving home, I cried so hard I could barely see what lane I was in; who the hell gets raped twice in their life? This time it was my fault! I shouldn't have been there, dammit. I pulled into the driveway, put the car in park, and raced into the house, past my mom, and to my bedroom. Finding a bottle of pills, I emptied handfuls into my mouth, swallowing as many as I could at once. I was done with life and didn't want to live anymore.

When my mom came into my room and discovered what I had done, she quickly called an ambulance. I prayed I would die before they got there. She called my grandpa, too. He arrived first. I told him everything, barely keeping my head up as the pills were kicking in; It disappointed him in me. It broke my heart knowing I had disappointed my grandpa.

When the ambulance arrived, I was almost incoherent. Picking me up from slouching over the kitchen table in a seated position, two paramedics carried me to the couch, where they stuck an IV in my arm.

"Just let me die," I muttered.

"Not today," a paramedic responded.

Blood splattered on the back of the wall, some on the couch, as a paramedic inserted an IV into my arm.

"Your blood is thinning. You could bleed to death internally," a paramedic spoke with concern to me. "Let's get you to the hospital."

They put me on a stretcher and carried me out of the house. While being put into the back of the ambulance, I glanced down with my hazy eyes to see Debbie and her parents gazing up at me. Her dad wanted to hunt Brian down and kill the son of a bitch. Debbie felt terrible. Debbie didn't know. Nobody knew. She never spoke to Brian again.

The nurses and doctor tried shoving a tube down my throat to use charcoal to flush out my stomach at the hospital. Clenching my teeth together, I damned near broke them, resisting the line. No way were they shoving that damn thing down my throat.

The police came in, threatening to take me to jail if I kept refusing the tube. I called their bluff, then replied, "If you can't get the contents from my stomach, you'll be taking me to the morgue instead." Even holding my nose closed; still, I wouldn't open my mouth. Starving for air, did these people not realize, suffocating me to death was only helping me out?

Finally, I gave in. The tube went down my throat, gagging the whole time it was horrific. The nurse emptied charcoal in it, telling me to keep it down.

A detective came into the room, wanting to get a statement from me. He said that they had Brian down at the station for questioning him. Even though they took semen samples from me when I first arrived at the hospital, Brian denied everything a pregnancy blood test. Thank God the bastard didn't get me pregnant.

The detective asks me questions the entire time; all I could think about is trying to keep the charcoal down. It was going to come up. I was trying so hard not to vomit. Closing my eyes, trying to breathe, and focus on his questions, three, two. One. I vomited right onto the detective's shoes. I then wondered if I had just committed an assault on a police officer. He peered at me, "no further questions." Then he left to go clean his shoes. I giggled a little. Staying in the hospital for the rest of the day, I finally got to go home that night. I went straight to my room and laid in my bed as my phone rang off the hook. Friends wanting to know if I was okay and wanting to know what happened. Wanting to be left alone, I laid in my bed, in the dark, wishing they would have just let me die.

Chapter Twenty-One
Time For A Change

I was lying low for a while, only working at the track, hanging out with my best friend, and a small group of other friends that I trusted. Everywhere I went, someone was pointing and talking behind my back. It was humiliating. The charges against Brian were dropped. The police closed the case believing it was a drunken teenage party that had just got out of control. The Justice system, at its finest, had failed me again. It was hard, but I gathered myself together, threw the bullshit behind me, trying to move on with my life. Shit was far from easy. It was a struggle.

Still working as a server, I met a dishwasher at the restaurant that was a new guy. We soon started dating. It was love at first sight. The only thing was,

I didn't know how to love someone.

I started changing once I dated Corey. I didn't notice it, but I was. I was pushing friends away from both of our lives. It was best for both of us. We had no good friends. They loved to party, and most were druggies. I was ready to break free from that lifestyle. It was getting rather old.

Whatever I told Corey to do, he would do it. I didn't notice right away that I was developing damaging behavior or destructive behavior at that matter. Jumping into a relationship after all I had been through wasn't such a great idea. I had had no time to heal. The healing process hadn't even taken place or so much as begun. I appeared to be vigorous on the outside, but I was a total catastrophe waiting to happen on the inside.

Victims/survivors are told to be strong, never give up fighting, that you are worth something, that what happened to you wasn't your fault—being taught to have the courage and some strength. To take something negative and turn it into something positive. I was never told to be positive or taught to be strong. I didn't know how to be. I had to live as if nothing ever happened, and life was always normal when it wasn't. I was just thrown into a mental health facility and locked away with many idiots paid to tell me they understood my anger and pain.

No the hell they didn't. I lived with the master of bull shitters my whole life. Did they think for one second they were going to bullshit with me?

My positive never showed. Sure, I laughed, had fun, and such. But I didn't know how to love or how to feel about it. Corey tried to love me. Love, to me, was just sex.

Tired of living in Corey's friend's basement, having no privacy, and all the partying that took place there, it was time to get our apartment. We had only been together for about four months when we made this decision. We found an apartment we could afford and didn't bother telling his friend was moving out of the basement. My preference was not to let anyone who partied or did drugs know where we were living. If Corey and I partied, it was mostly by ourselves or with a small group of friends we trusted, and that group was tiny.

I didn't know it, but I was showing signs of trouble lying ahead of triggers, too. I didn't know what either was or meant. I had no proper care or healing. If someone grabbed or touched me in some particular way, it would instantly generate fury, rage, and so much anger that I would black out, petrifying whoever angered me—leaving that person as to having no clue what they had done.

Sometimes, I would even cringe if Corey kissed or touched me. Sometimes, I wouldn't. Certain smells, words, mood swings, bad tempers, getting fired from jobs or just quitting them for no reason, and one hell of a poor attitude.

The longer Corey and I lived together, the more controlling I became. He had a job and paid the bills while I continued to work at the Go-Kart track. It was the only job I could keep. My friends were there, and all the customers were like family.

It was one of my "happy places."

When I wasn't a raging psycho, Corey and I got along really great. We had little money, but we did things that were cheap and shopped cheap, shared lots of laughs, spending time loving one another. Sometimes I was tense and panicky that Corey might have some sort of side he hid that would make an appearance, breaking out and harm me. He always reassured me he would never do such a thing; he made a promise and kept it. With him, I felt safe. He knew about my past. It made him sick to his stomach. He never wanted to hear me talk about it, though. I had to bottle it up and tuck it away. It had to be a secret with him.

I wasn't allowed to talk to anyone about it. It wasn't right; it was my story; it was what happened to me. Guessing the apple doesn't fall far from the tree, Corey and I would get into arguments. I would throw shit, break shit, and push him, sometimes even hitting him. He knew how to push my buttons, getting under my skin, make it crawl.

When I became angry, it wasn't a "normal" angry. I would just blackout, going into a rage. What Corey didn't understand was, I had no respect for men.

My behavior was becoming controlling, too.

Corey wasn't allowed to do much of anything without my permission. If he didn't get my license, there was a shouting match, and the rage and anger put itself on display again. My hairline would be sweaty after calming down, and I would be out of breath and exhausted. Most of all, I would repeatedly apologize for becoming out of control. He always accepted my apologies. Then we would act as if nothing ever happened. He would allow me to get away with this. I was an enormous train wreck. The worst part, I was an abuse victim that was now abusing. Shit was just beginning. It was going to continue to get more detrimental.

Chapter Twenty-Two
First Sweet, Then Sour

New Year's Eve 1994, Corey and I went out to a friend's house and partied to bring in the new year. We had an exciting time and a few too many. I was a sucker for champagne! To me, a new year meant new and better things to come. I only hoped. We stumbled into our small one-bedroom apartment and went to bed just a little after 1 a.m.

Weeks went by; I started getting sick. Every morning I woke up feeling like death, hugging the bathroom toilet, begging for mercy, praying to God, Jesus, and the heavens above. Becoming a little suspicious, Corey took me to a clinic. It came back that I was pregnant. Walking out of the clinic, I was young, only eighteen, but we were both shocked and happy at the same time. I noticed I had a little extra bounce to my step for the first time in a long time and was grinning from ear to ear.

My mom was in shock. But I told her to buckle down; whether she liked it, a baby was coming. Corey's parents weren't shocked at all since we were living together.

Corey and I sat down and had a long talk. We had to weed out all our bad friends, and all the party life was over. It was time to grow up. I didn't want my baby growing up in an unfit home the way I grew up. My baby was going to have a better life than I did. I made it clear to him when we started communicating about marriage, and the baby wasn't getting his last name unless we were married. Being an unwed mother didn't sit right with me. We also had to talk about getting home. I couldn't raise a baby in a one-bedroom apartment. So much was thrown on our plate at once. We didn't know where to start.

I couldn't work with all the sickness from being pregnant. It wasn't just morning sickness; it lasted twenty-four hours a day, never knowing when I was going to throw up again or what food or smell was going to make me nauseous. It was terrible.

We had crappy furniture, a tiny TV, an old wobbly kitchen table. I must have inherited furnishing apartments from that bastard I called "my dad." My mood swings were worse than ever, causing Corey and me almost to cancel our small two-hundred-dollar backyard wedding in July. We would have been together one year by the time we were married. We moved fast. I was going to be almost six months pregnant at my wedding dress, but I didn't care. Corey bought a nice trailer off my aunt in the country in a trailer park. It was better than living in an apartment with more space, two bedrooms, and a fenced-in yard for the baby to play. The next-door neighbors were jackasses, and we didn't get along with them. It was our only problem.

My mood swings were becoming more frequent and violent. We thought they were from pregnancy hormones and blew them off as being just that. When I came down from my rages, God, I was so exhausted. Felt as if I had run a marathon. We thought they would mellow out once I had the baby.

It was exasperating being at home all the time. My friends were all out partying, and I was home pregnant, married, starting a family. Still working the track on the weekends, I found a part-time job at a mortgage company—a bad idea. I just wanted out of the house and extra money for me, Corey, and the baby. There was a co-worker there that was testing my patience daily. Giving her more than a fair warning, she pushed me too far one day, and I picked a chair up and smashed it against her. Of course, they fired me. No shits were given. I felt as if it spent me with putting up with people's shit, but I was spiraling out of control. It was only going to keep getting more inferior.

Corey ended up getting a great job at a local college as a Grounds Keeper. It paid great, so we didn't have to worry about money. We spent his weekend shopping and decorating the baby's room. Finding out we were having a girl, we decorated her room in my favorite television show when I was a kid, Sesame Street. It turned out well. Cute! Corey and I were getting along better, and he spoiled me every chance he got.

That was a bonus.

After working the track one night in

October, we came home, and no sooner than I sat down on the couch, I went into full-blown labor.

Gripping the carpet on my hands and knees, Corey called my mom, and off to the hospital, we went! I was not a pleasant woman to be around! Seven hours later, we had our baby girl, Katie. She was beautiful. I held her in my arms, staring at her with tears in my eyes. As I held this precious baby, I thought about all the things that dad had done to me when I was that little, throwing me like some object. I couldn't imagine doing that to my baby girl. I knew Corey wouldn't dare harm her, but I clarified that if he ever did, I would kill him. My kids would never see the pain that I had known and felt. It was a promise, a promise I would keep, not one of my dad's crappy, lying promises.

Katie and I were healthy and discharged from the hospital the next day. I brought her home in her car seat, placed her on the kitchen counter, stared at her as she slept, and thought, "what do I do now?" I giggled to myself. Being a young mother, I was nineteen when she was born; I wasn't sure what to do with her next, but I knew I would figure it out. Motherly instinct would kick in.

The first night Katie was home, she was up every two hours crying. I wasn't expecting this.

Every two hours like clockwork, she was up screaming, wanting to be fed. I was exhausted. I let Corey sleep because he was the breadwinner and had to work in the morning. Katie would scream. She screamed a lot. However, I kept my patience with her. Later, I found out she had colic and had to be on a unique formula. She still cried, but that was expected, but at least she wasn't screaming every waking hour.

Every chance I had, I showed off my baby girl. I was so proud of this little human being that I made. So precious and innocent. And I finally had someone that would love me unconditionally. Mom became a proud grandma and would snatch Katie up on Saturday nights to give me a break. We were getting along a little better, but still had our quarrels.

Corey and I fought always again. I was becoming more aggressive, defiant, and combative. Up all night with a baby left me even more irritable. I was a ticking time bomb, and the switch could fire up quickly, activating me into terrible temper tantrums, and you never knew it was forthcoming. I was kind of like a crackerjack box; you never knew what you were going to get inside.

I was always "sorry" after my "blackout tantrums" and pissed because I broke stuff in the home that took money to replace and repair. Then there was Corey. I abused him physically, mentally, and emotionally. My mood swings were physically and mentally draining the shit out of me; I didn't know why. I lay in bed at night after putting Katie to sleep, holding her on my chest, embracing her, giving her soft head kisses that smelled so good of baby lotion. I was suffering from a lot of headaches, sometimes nausea. Migraines that I had since I was a child were becoming more frequent and intense. My body would ache sometimes, and I would get sick often. If I caught a virus, everyone else would have it for a day or two; I would have it for weeks or over a month. My body seemed as if it was having a challenging time fighting off illnesses.

Starting a new family and struggling to strive in life seemed almost impossible. Sometimes I would lie in bed at night in my silent house. I would think about all the problems dad put me through—the horror, the terror, all of it.

Hearing the baby cry from her crib on the baby monitor, I did what an average, loving, and caring parent would do. I got out of bed and strolled quietly to her room, being sure not to wake Corey; he had to be at work early the next morning.

I made baby Katie a bottle, then strolled back into her room, nestling her against my chest. Sitting down in the rocking chair, I placed her bottle in her mouth, rocking back and forth. Her little brown eyes stared at me, comforting me when I needed it the most. I kissed the top of her head, then sang to her, "Hush, little baby, don't say a word." I stopped singing. "Wrong song choice," I mumbled.

Chapter Twenty-Three
The Warning Signs

In March 1996, I found out I was pregnant again. This time I was having a little boy! Once again, I was excited. No matter how shitty of a day I was having, my kids made me happy. They were the light to the dark tunnel I had hidden in for so long—a reason to wake up and be strong every morning.

And for once, I didn't want to die. I was always sick with this pregnancy, too. It was hard for me. But I knew it would be well worth it in the end.

The day after Christmas, I went into the hospital to get induced. Six hours later, my son, Cody, was born. Just like my daughter, who was now fourteen months old, he was perfect!

After Cody was born, there were other things that I did I could not control. I didn't know why I did them, but I did, and later in life, I would find out why. Taking out massive amounts of credit cards, going on spending sprees, buying the kids every toy imaginable, furniture, and vehicles we could not afford every day was something. We were drowning in debt because of my habit. I wanted to live the champagne lifestyle on a beer budget. My behavior was dismissed as cruel, rude, hateful, neglectful, and so forth. Warning signs were shooting off like fireworks on the fourth of July that there was something wrong with me. It's not like we ignored it. We just didn't know. Nobody knew. I was jumping into my little world of self-destruction. I never wanted to think that the old bastard I used to call my "dad" think he had won by ripping my insides apart. I felt nothing for Corey anymore. I didn't even know why. I couldn't explain it. He did nothing wrong. All I cared about, loved, and appreciated were my two babies. The ones I would keep safe and do no harm. As I gazed at my sweet angels sleeping, I whispered, "I love you. You are my life."

A few months after having Cody, I went back to school and got my GED. I then enrolled in college to pursue a degree in nursing. In the evening, I went to school, worked during the day as a CNA (Certified Nursing Assistant), did all the housework, grocery shopping, taking care of two babies; it was just becoming too overwhelming. I was lucky if I had enough time to get my homework or studying done. It was draining me, and Corey was of no help. He wasn't very supportive. If I lifted myself the slightest, he would bring me back down. That was one of his faults that I could not stand.

He was a pretty negative person. He complained about everything. That was what would send me spiraling out of control. He would bring the worst out of me. All he was doing was pushing me away.

Working many jobs, I was getting fired for calling in too much because I didn't have a babysitter or couldn't afford one; I worked nights so Corey could keep the babies while I worked. I had a few bad babysitters as well. With them being with Corey, I didn't have to worry about them so much. By then, I had turned twenty-one. I found a job as a server at a bar, and the money was excellent. The only problem was, I found out was I was missing out on the adult party lifestyle. I was introduced to the partying atmosphere that I had worked so hard to escape from a few years back.

After my shifts - clocking out, staying late, drinking, partying, dancing, and flirting with older men were so intoxicating. Not trying to sound like a narcissist, but I had bloomed into a beautiful young woman, and the men were continually flirting, chasing, or offering me the world. I called bullshit. A man can tell a thousand lies; I had learned my lesson well with the lies that rolled off their tongues. Playing along for the attention was just a game to me. It scored more money at the end of my shifts, too.

The fights between Corey and me were damn near daily. He didn't want me working at a bar. "It's no place for a married mother," he would snap at me.

"I'll do whatever the hell I want," I would spit back.

"You're going to work dressed like that," he would sarcastically question.

"What? Now you can tell me what I can and can't wear," I would angrily reply. My tone would then soften as I kissed my babies' goodbye and then turned to give Corey the middle finger salute before I strolled out the front door, slamming it behind me.

One night, I came home from work, told Corey some lame excuse that I was getting a promotion at work and had to attend a meeting. I took a shower, got dressed up, and left. My boss and I had developed a crush on each other and had an affair.

Corey followed me that night and found out. Confessing the truth, Corey packed his shit and left. It was the first time I had ever felt terrible for doing something awful towards Corey. All he ever tried to do was to love me. Nothing he ever did was good enough. I felt like nothing I ever did was good enough, either. I don't know why I committed the ultimate betrayal in marriage; I couldn't explain why I did. Luckily, Corey and I could work things out, and he forgave me, coming back home wanting to be a family again. I quit my job at the bar. Staying home with the kids and being taking care of the family became a priority. Despite all the bullshit, my kids were always the top priority. The only matter they suffered from was hearing mommy and daddy arguing a lot. Knowing it wasn't right for them, I did everything in my God-forsaken power to keep my outbursts and temper at bay.

Corey and I never spoke of the affair again; the fighting died down, only arguing now and then.

The kids were happy and even happier when Corey and I sold the trailer and rented a cute little house in a small town that my parents grew up in. The town had great schools and old town traditions, too. Great place to raise a family. The same small town that dad picked us up in before shit hit the fan. Here I was, going back.

The kids loved it! Katie was about three years old, and Cody was two. The house sat on a quiet cul-de-sac where the kids could ride their bikes, an excellent babysitter, and a sheriff lived across the street. There were even kids their age to play with. Perfect.

Our new landlord was a very nice old man, even put Corey to work, taking it out of our rent money, with money to pay some of our bills left over. He owned over eighty properties. By then, Corey had picked up the painting trade from my stepdad so Corey painted rentals on the side. Even more perfect.

Matters seemed to get better for the family, but I kept it hidden that I wasn't happy. Yes, my kids made me happy. But it's a different happiness, one that is hard to explain. As you're trying to move on with your life, you have this uneasy feeling that you can't describe, hanging over you or building inside of you. It's lurking. You can't tell anyone because you don't know what it is. That "thing" that was lurking inside me was just causing trouble for me. Brushing it under the rug always was going to turn into many disasters and one massive fucking catastrophe. God, if I only knew.

Chapter Twenty-Four
Another Train Wreck

I became quite a little homemaker in our new home. Spending quality time with the kids, grocery shopping, cooking, cleaning, planting flower beds, mowing grass, and did I mention that my shopping habit had returned? Corey found out and took my bank card. The situation sent me into an outrage. He only gave me enough money to get groceries every week. That didn't fly with me. Telling Corey, I picked up a job at a family restaurant at night; I had even welled plans in mind. The "don't mess with me" switch was once again turned on inside my fucked-up mind.

A friend of mine was a stripper dancer, whatever you want to call it. She made great money and could support herself and her children on her own. She had a friendly lifestyle. Figuring why not, I told Corey I was leaving for work, and off I went to work with her.

Sauntering into the club, it was dark. Neon lights lit up the horseshoe-shaped bar, the bartender wearing "barely anything," was slinging drinks to a bunch of perverted old men, whose eyes were gazing without a blink at the half-naked young girl twirling around the pole on stage.

Grabbing my friend by the arm as she led me to the dressing room, "Leah, I am nervous" I said. "You? Nervous about something?" She threw her head back and laughed, dragging me into the dressing room, helping me get ready to make my first appearance as a half-naked chick, twirling around a pole on stage.

Stepping out, my name was called over the speaker. I just went by my real name, Lindsey.

With white high-heeled boots that came up to the knees, a short white see-through skirt, and a white see-through tank that tied together in the front, showing off my toned tummy, I strolled onto the stage, waiting for the music to play. "Purple Rain" by Prince- what I had chosen. My eyes closed, I took a deep breath, felt the music, and danced on that stage like I had been working there for years. Every patron in the club had all eyes on me, requesting lap dances when I was through.

Passing Leah, "Girl, that dance to that song took my breath away." She nudged me.

"Thanks," I beamed a smile, striding back to the dressing room. My shift was over, and I had a wad of cash. It was a great night, although I did smell of about fifty different perverted men's cologne.

Corey eventually caught me working as a stripper. Working a shift, I was on stage, and when I looked over, he was sitting at the end staring at me. My heart raced, and I was speechless. Corey burned my stripper clothes on the backyard grill, so my stripper days were over. What always boggled my mind about the whole stripper thing, I was the only one that could get on stage completely sober. The rest of the girls were drunk or high or both.

Corey continued to keep my bank card, so I found a job at a busy family owned breakfast restaurant. The money was excellent.

We could afford to do more things with the kids. Take small family trips and move into a bigger rental home. Our landlord was nice enough to breakdown and allowed us to get a family dog. She was the sweetest, most obedient dog ever. We loved her so much.

Corey and I fought little anymore, either. Of course, there wasn't much time for it. As the kids grew older, there was soccer, softball, basketball, after school events, on top of me working. The kids and I kept busy; Corey was in a world of his own.

We nominated Friday nights as family nights. The kids and I enjoyed them. Corey? Not so much. He bitched the whole time. It got old, really fucking old. My brother graduated from high school. I didn't make it to the graduation because there wasn't enough room and you had to have a ticket. So, we stopped by the party at my mom's house instead. We pulled up to the front yard, parking along the side of the curb.

There were already so many people filling the house. A big yard sign stood out in the middle of the yard, "Congratulations, Jake," in his school colors of red and white. Me, Corey, and the kids stepped out of the car, hiked up the bright green grass, and into the front door of mom's home. Crowds of people stood or wandered everywhere.

I went upstairs to the kitchen to give my brother his graduation card, with Corey and the kids following close behind me.

I stopped in my tracks; my mouth gaped, my body felt weak, and I trembled sweat beads built upon my forehead as nausea kicked in my tummy. Gazing at my mom, raising a brow, I wanted to say, "What the hell is my dad doing here?" The words wouldn't come out of my mouth. Dad was leaning against the kitchen counter, one leg crossed over the other, with his new wife, yes, she had children. He was leaning as if his crap didn't stink.

Looking in the opposite direction, giving mom the look of death, out the corner of my eye, I could feel his eyes digging into me. "Say, something bastard. I'm not a frightened little girl anymore. I will devour you. Make your wish they locked you up, fried you, for everything you did to me. Too bad, they were just thoughts.

Giving my brother his card, I wanted to walk out but the kids had spotted the cake. I allowed them to have some before we left. The sharp look of death never withdrew from mom the entire time I was there. She pulled me aside. "He just wanted to come to his son's open house," she said like it was no big damn deal. I was so angry I wanted to cry. He only raped your daughter, you know?

I gritted my teeth in rage. I walked away, grabbed my kids, and left. I told Corey I didn't want to talk about or hear another word about it on the way home. I just gazed out the window, feeling like I wasn't worth anything! I didn't even know half of the shit I was going to find out later. Lots of betrayals. God, I hate that son of a bitch.

Chapter Twenty-Five
The Worst Parts Are Still To Come

In December 2002, I found out I was pregnant again. A few months later, we found out I was having another boy. We were so excited; even the kids couldn't wait for their new baby brother. I was twenty-five by then.

When I had our precious boy, I fell ill after delivery. Shaking, vomiting, sweating, tunnel vision, and a sudden drop in blood pressure. The nurses came running in to get me back to normal. After declaring Nick healthy and me, we were discharged the next day. We found something to be a little odd, though. I was engorging myself in chocolate.

I could not stop eating it, and I had never been much of a sweet eater before. We just shook it off. My rages were slowly returning, and I was getting sick often again. I even caught pneumonia so bad one time I had it for over a month. It hurt so bad I couldn't move out of bed. My immune system had become weak. My blood pressure was always low, sometimes so low it was hard to stand up. The doctor blew it off, which would later become a big mistake. All these matters would start adding up along with the rages and blackouts. Spending sprees, too.

Playing supermom, I worked, picked the kids up from the sitters, came home, cleaned, helped with homework, did the grocery shopping, took them to their sporting events, music lessons, all the things moms do. I was exhausted, running on very little sleep, living off caffeine and cigarettes, and my body was feeling worn down, but I kept ongoing. I stayed active and kept the kids occupied as well. Katie was in travel, softball, and basketball, so we were gone a lot. It turns out that Cody wasn't only a great soccer player but; he found a guitar that I had received from Corey for Christmas, swearing I would learn how to play it. With my busy schedule, I never understood. Cody picked it up. Within minutes, he was playing by ear along with the radio! We were all shocked. He ended up dropping soccer for guitar lessons to learn to read music; the boy was amazing.

On top of everything else I was doing, Cody was becoming one hell of a musician. We learned he could play pretty much any instrument, including piano, that he could get his hands on. My son could even sing. He started his band. He was struggling to get shows, so I stepped up and helped him by managing the band. It was bearing more weight on my shoulders, but I would do anything for my kids.

Balancing having a family, my daughter's schedule with softball and basketball, taking care of a young son, who was now about five, who played soccer, went to kindergarten, managed a band, worked a job, and then came helping my husband run his own painting business. I had also developed a severe case of OCD and was very tedious when it came to the house and the yard. I wouldn't allow anyone else to clean it, so it all had to be done by me. I was asleep by the time my head hit the pillow late at night and up at the crack of dawn.

Even though I didn't think about what had happened to me in the past, they still weighed heavy in the back of my mind. With not healing from what happened to me, stress, not eating right, or some days not eating at all because I didn't have time, running a rat race all over the place, working, and playing "perfect mom," there was a bomb inside me with a fuse. That fuse was about to be lit, exploding, and shit was going to hit the fan in the worse way I could ever imagine.

Chapter Twenty-Six
Normal

The stress of taking care of ninety percent of things was wearing me down quickly. I was appearing as if I was a walking skeleton; my clothes were hanging off me. But it didn't stop me, always on the go. Corey's excuses were still, "I have to work," but I would always come home and catch him with his feet up. He would act as if he just got home. I just shook my head to avoid any conflict. Corey loved conflict, and I hated my rages. He would send me into a frenzy, then act as if he did nothing wrong. There were a lot of matters going on between us again. You could cut the tension in the air with a knife sometimes. He always acted as if I couldn't survive a day without him - Pfft, please! One less person to wait on hand and foot.

Trivial things started adding up that he would do or allow started bothering me.

People would slander me behind my back, and he wouldn't stick up for me, or he would do business behind my back when we were supposed to be business partners. Corey pissed off a lot of customers; some I saved, some I couldn't. He ran his business in the ground when I walked away from it a few times because I couldn't deal with his bullshit anymore. When he had no business, he would sit at home and wait for the phone to ring, hello? It would help if you worked to get the phone to ring. Knowing I had kids to feed and a roof to keep over our heads, I would go back into the office, work, and get the phone ringing again. It made me cringe doing anything for him. He wasn't even thankful. He would look at it as if it were "my duty as a parent," when all I had to do is get a job outside the home, pack my shit, take the kids and leave. If I knew what was to come, I wouldn't have been such a dumbass and stayed! I was becoming a train wreck again, and it showed.

Spending a lot of time at my son's guitar and drum lessons at a local lesson center, my son ended up joining a second band as their drummer. He was now in two bands. Being that I was there a lot, I met and became friends with just about everyone that worked there. Two of the teachers and I became good friends. One of them—I'll call him Max—became friends with me on social media. We would chat while I did office work. I even did this in front of Corey. Our computer was out in the open, and there was no hiding anything. Corey was fully aware. He wanted me to end it. End what? A friendship? Then he threatened to tell the man's wife - after I found out he had placed spyware on the computer that recorded everything I did or typed on the computer all day. So, what? He invaded my privacy, not that I had anything to hide, but I sure as hell packed my shit up and left for his crazy ass bullshit, filed for a divorce, and stayed at my parents. He threatened to tell Max's wife we were having an affair. It could have cost the man his marriage. Corey had lost his damned mind! Of course, after about a month, I withdrew the divorce filing and went back home. After a few days, life resumed back to normal, well, at least for a while. Ready or not, here it comes. Shit was about to hit the fan! Life as I knew it would never be the same.

Chapter Twenty-Seven
What's Happening To Me

I'm the only kid between my siblings and me that can tell you what struggle, tragedy, heartache, fear, numbness, and real pain feels like, what the overwhelming feeling of waking up every day wanting to die feels like. I have never felt loved enough, fair enough, or felt like I was a "somebody." Even though I have anger issues, I am tough on the outside, but I have a heart and feelings. People like me don't see color anymore; we only see black or white. We are also intimidated easily and never let our guard down, sometimes even keeping our circle small because of trust issues. Later, I was going to find out that the people I never thought would betray me were the ones who betrayed me the most.

Working at the bar again, I was the breakfast server, but this time, I was there to make money and have somewhat of a social life outside of being a mom and a wife. The customers were thrilled to see me working there again.

One Monday morning, we were very slow, having only one customer. Jed, the cook, and I was sitting at the bar drinking a coke, chatting, and he brought up a segment that he had watched on

Dateline the previous night.

It was on child pedophiles. He said they interviewed a hillbilly pedophile in prison that said, "I ain't no "pedophiler." We both had a great laugh at the way he pronounced pedophile.

Since my dad doesn't even deserve the title of being called "dad," for the rest of this book, he will be known as "pedophiler." It suits him very well.

Between the kids and all their activities, managing a band, running a business, taking care of a house, working a job, and so much more, I was becoming "high strung," very stressed out, and not taking excellent care of myself at all. I was starting not to feel very well, either. Life can change in a second. I was already aware of this.

What I didn't know was that matters were about to get worse for me. A lot worse. And like with the "pedophiler," I didn't see it coming. My new nightmare was about to begin.

Chapter Twenty-Eight
The New Nightmare Begins

In January 2012, I felt worn down. The fatigue I was experiencing was terrible, along with frequent migraines, headaches, and mood swings with rages showing its ugly face again. Not only that, everyone kept thinking I was hiding a pregnancy because my belly was round and protruding out. I appeared as if I was nine months pregnant. It was weird. As much as I loved my job at the bar, it was becoming way too much for me, and I had to quit. I wanted to cry but trying to juggle everything I was doing was destroying my health, and physically, I was past the point of exhaustion.

Hell, in the years since I have been alive, I could never relax or take any time for "me." I don't know what either of those words means. I think I am the only woman in the world that has never even had her nails done! Too busy taking care of everyone else my whole life, I forgot to take care of myself. The bomb was lit, and it was about to go off.

I spent the summer with the kids, swimming at my mom's; she had her in-ground pool. The kids would swim while I tanned. We went out to eat, go to the fairs, shop, and go to an amusement park with my husband, parents, sister, and kids.

On the way home, it was dark, and I drove my van. I damned near killed us all on the interstate. I became confused for a moment, then my vision blurred, almost causing me to wreck into a semi-truck, then a cement barricade. I do not know how the hell I saved us from that wreck. We had an angel watching over us that night—more weird symptoms. I wasn't sure if I should tell anyone or just keep it to myself. I did mention a little to my mother. Nothing more was said after I told her.

We had a great summer. Little did I know, that would be the last summer I would ever get to spend living like a normal human being. Everything I loved was about to be taken away. Why me?

In December 2012, I was stressed out as I usually was, just like every Christmas season. You never knew if you would have enough work or not, and work was prolonged with having a business. We ended up fortunate, and my husband received a call about a tremendous job that paid great, causing me to finally breathe easily until I found out who the job was contracted through. My husband's contractor would work for was very well known to screw over his subs and the homeowners. He had changed his business's name many times and was not in good standing with the Better Business Bureau. He had a horrible reputation. My husband convinced me that he would make sure he got paid, so I finally gave in and trusted Corey to make sure he would get his money from the slime ball. The closer it came to Christmas, bills were not getting paid, and there was nothing under the tree for the kids. This was making me a nervous wreck. Not a single dime was coming in. The slime ball was bullshitting around on the job, not getting things done, and fucking around. The homeowner was not happy either, and subs were not getting paid. I knew this was going to happen. I told Corey to get what was owed to him. I was angry and wasn't experimenting with this slime ball.

No matter what Corey did, he couldn't get his money. Do you know what that means?

Don't get the angry wife involved.

Calling and texting, the slime ball kept switching dates on when he was going to pay. Then the idiot wanted me to talk to his wife, who had left him, and convinced her to go back home. What the hell? I wanted my money. When did I become a marriage counselor? This guy is nuts.

Finally, I threatened to blast his ass on social media if he didn't pay up within twenty-four hours. He finally did. No sooner than the money was in my hands, I was out the door to buy Christmas for my kids and trying to get back into the Christmas spirit and do all the traditions we did throughout the years. The slime ball ruined half of the holiday season; I would not allow him to destroy the rest.

On my way out the door, I threw an exasperated stare over at Corey. "If I want something done, I have to do it myself," I hollered, slamming the front door behind me.

Chapter Twenty-Nine
Welcome To My New Nightmare

Luckily, I could find the right parking spot at the overly crowded mall. I was happy since I didn't have to walk so far in the brutal Indiana cold to get inside the warm over-crowded mall. I wish I could have avoided. I was not a last-minute person. I always did things ahead of time. Due to slime balls bull crap, I was now stressed out and stuck doing last-minute Christmas shopping in an overcrowded mall, which is not suitable for a person with severe anger issues and no fucking patience. I was hoping whatever I said or did while shopping would not be held against me in the court of law.

Standing in one of my oldest son's favorite stores, I was trying to decide what shoes to purchase for him. "Damn. Why is everything so expensive," I was thinking to myself. "Bills, Christmas, bills, Christmas, bills…" I was also thinking. My mind was spinning in circles. Suddenly, I didn't feel so good. My heart did a couple of flips in my chest, and beads of sweat formed upon my forehead. My body felt weak and began to shake and tremble. My stomach felt nauseous, and I had tunnel vision; I thought I was going to faint. Sauntering over to the counter near the cashier, I leaned against the counter to get myself together. "Are you okay," she questioned with concern. "You look pale."

"I'm fine. Just a sugar crash. Have had nothing to eat today," I lied.

"Okay. Just checking." She continued to work, and I bought the shoes I finally picked out and left the store.

I continued shopping, feeling like death, my symptoms never went away, but I hung in there and get what I needed to be done. I then raced to the van, tossed all the bags in the back, leaped in, and drove like a Nascar driver all the way home. Once I arrived, I grabbed my bags from the back, made a dash for the house, damn near ripping the front door off the hinges, threw the gears in my bedroom, kicked off my shoes, and threw myself onto the couch as everyone stared at me. I then told Corey everything that happened. We agreed either I had caught some sort of virus or had been so stressed out that I just needed some rest. Corey took care of matters for the day while I spent the day sleeping on and off on the couch. The symptoms never went away that day. It was awful. Tomorrow was a new day, right?

The next morning, I awoke to feel worse than I had the day before. Rolling over to the edge of my bed, sitting up, I felt as if an eighteen wheeler and drug had hit me about one-hundred feet! With no rest from the night before, my heart flipping in my chest, my body shook and trembled to the bone so severely, it shook the mattress and, my entire Whitaker bed.

Scuffling my feet down the long hallway and turning into the kitchen, the left side of my body trembled, the nausea was gagging me. I took my first sip of coffee. A powerful tremor took over my body, it appeared as if I was having a seizure, but I was awake. As much as I love my coffee in the morning, the cup went into the sink. I shed a few tears, watching the liquid gold flow down the drain. I know you all feel me.

Corey strode into the kitchen, and I told him what had just happened and how sickly I had felt—trying not to worry anyone, because even though Corey and I had our arguments and hardened times when I complained of being sick of something, he showed a lot of care for me. I was never one to complain about being sick. Hell, I could have the flu, scarlet fever, yellow fever, mumps, measles, shingles, chickenpox, and strep, and still run a household. Not with this shit. Something wasn't right. I could feel it. Without the kids being in a distance where they could hear me, I whispered to Corey,

"Something isn't right. I'll give it a few days just to make sure it's not a virus. But something isn't right." Staring at him, locking eyes with him, I was so pale I could feel it.

"I have noticed you have been getting dark circles around your eyes, and the bridge of your nose looks bruised lately. I can see that you're pale. You don't look good," he responded with concern.

I leaned against the kitchen counter, feeling weak. "I have noticed, too," I whispered. "I'm going to go take a hot shower and see if it helps."

Leaving the kitchen, I went and took a hot shower. Completely drained after my shower, I couldn't believe a simple shower had caused me so much fatigue. I got myself dressed, brushed my hair and teeth, then laid in bed watching TV, spending the next few hours trying to get some stamina back.

Chapter Thirty

Emergency Rooms And Doctors, Oh My

We went to Wal-Mart later that day to do a little more shopping. Even though I was not well, I went along.

Stepping out the front door, the winter sunlight caught my eyes, making them hurt like hell, barely being able to open them to see. My body trembled, my heart flipped, and the nausea was almost unbearable. My body felt even weaker. After everything I had been through in my life, I was a pretty tough cookie, so I toughed it out and trudged to the van, getting inside, strapping my seatbelt on, placing my sunglasses over my painful eyes, plastering my head to the back of the seat, and praying to the heavens above to get me through the trip.

Upon arriving at Wal-Mart, the further we trekked to the store's back, my symptoms became worse. In the toy aisle, peering down at some toys on a bottom shelf, I went off into some "trance."

Corey tried getting my attention; once I came out of it, he said it was time to go to the emergency room.

He explained what I had done on the way out of the store. I remembered nothing.

When we arrived at the emergency room and spoke to them about my symptoms, they thought I had a mini-stroke, rushing me back.

I didn't look so good. The doctor performed a small bundle of tests on me; everything came back normal, except my blood pressure was once again low. There would explain that later. The doctor strolled into the room, giving me a prescription for Xanax, explaining that he was pretty sure I had anxiety and panic attacks. I didn't even know what the hell those were. And As far as Xanax went, I had never taken a pill in my life. Only amoxicillin whenever I had strep or an ear infection. I heard this was terrible shit. Slipping the prescription into my purse, I peered at Corey, "Get me out of here." We headed home, not knowing that matters were only going to get worse. Much worse.

A few weeks went by, and my symptoms were intensifying; more appeared. I lost my appetite, and what I could eat when I did would just sit in my stomach and not digest. Vomiting it up a few days later, yep, it didn't summarize. My belly was extended more than ever, with a deformed shape to it. My heart repeatedly flipped, along with all the other symptoms I explained before. Migraines so painful and debilitating thought my skull was going to split wide open. I only got out of bed to make the millions of trips to the emergency rooms. I was bouncing around to all of them, hoping someone had a clue what was going on. The fatigue was horrific, along with the muscle weakness, I could barely make it to the shower or brush my teeth. The emergency rooms kept making me feel even worse when I left and writing those fucking prescriptions for Xanax that went through the paper shredder when I arrived home. I wasn't taking some stupid pill that I didn't need.

I would rock back and forth in my bed when I was having what I called "an episode," where I would get the sweating, tunnel vision, heart flipping, and so forth it would last for hours. I hated going to the doctor. As sick as I was, I wished they made house calls. I broke down and call the family doctor and get myself in to see her with all hopes she knew what was going on with me.

Not being able to so much as to drive myself anywhere because of my symptoms, my mom picked me up for my doctor's appointment. On the way there, I peered out the window, staring at the fields of melting snow, wondering why such cruel things always had to happen to me. What did I ever do to deserve the shit that was continually being dished out to me? I could only take so much.

Mom dropped me off at the doctor's office's front door, and she waited in the car as I went inside. I was a chaotic mess, and people were staring. No shits were given.

Of course, when you are sick, they hand you a clipboard of paperwork wanting to know everything, including your relatives that lived back in the 1820s blood type.

Filling out the paperwork, trembling, nauseous, I just wanted to throw the clipboard and run to the car to head back home. The nurse called me back before I could finish plotting my escape, weighed me then took me to a room.

Explaining to the nurse why I was there (I don't know why because I would have to explain them again when the doctor came in), she asked me some questions, then left, telling me the doctor would see me shortly. We all know "shortly" means you should have brought your camping equipment; the doctor will leave you sitting here sick all freaking day. So, I waited, and waited, and waited, oh yeah, I waited some more.

An hour later (see, I told you) the doctor came in, and since I went to one of those (I have no health insurance, so you get what kind of shitty doctor you can get plans,) I was curious what she could come up with.

Feeling like a broken record, going through my symptoms again, she asked about my stress levels, past medical history, and so forth. She then told me that I had a panic and anxiety disorder, gave me a prescription for Xanax and a therapist's phone number. The bitch was out of her mind! Had she been talking to the emergency rooms? I shuffled out of there, only to go home, lay in bed, and my symptoms become more miserable by the day. And with each passing day, new ones appeared. It was getting out of control. So, I had to break down and make another appointment with Dr. Panic Disorder.

At my second appointment, Dr. Panic Disorder was sure that I had the disorder, but some of my symptoms weren't adding up with the disease, even though others were. She became a little baffled, pulling out her laptop, beginning to google. My eyes damn near bulged out of their sockets when she googled. You're charging me what? To google a diagnosis. Hell, I have been in the wrong fucking business! I was googling my symptoms at home, and it kept coming up that I was dying, so I quit googling.

Dr. Panic Disorder, with the help of "Google," diagnosed me with Meniere's Disease.

Vertigo, dizziness, nausea, and migraines were signs of this disease. Feeling optimistic because I wanted a diagnosis and cure so severely, I went along with it. She referred me to an ENT.

No sooner than I arrived home, I made the appointment to get into the ENT. Several weeks later, still bedridden and miserable, we went in, and the ENT tested me for Meniere's Disease. Filled with disappointment, it was not what was wrong with me. I left the office with no diagnosis, no cure. Not a word was spoken from my mouth on the drive home. Sauntering into the house, I went to my bedroom, lay down in my bed, bursting into tears. So sick and miserable, "why the hell me?"

Chapter Thirty-One
Are You Trying To Kill Me, Doc

Doctor Panic Disorder became more baffled with each visit, as my symptoms were growing. I was so sick I could barely hold my head up. She referred me to a great neurologist, and when I called to make the appointment, the waiting list was nine months. Even when I explained to them my condition, the receptionist couldn't squeeze me in. So, the wait began, the misery continued.

The worst part of being sick was "feeling guilty." Katie and Cody were teenagers in high school, Nick in elementary school, just turning nine-years-old. Corey and the two oldest kids were doing everything they could to keep the house and other matters together, but they were so used to me running things, everything was falling apart. There was so much to do, and I just couldn't do it. Nick wasn't getting the attention and time with me that the other two got when growing up.

The guilt of that matter weighed down my shoulders, too. Frustration and depression were now making an appearance. Not being able to take care of your family, house, and kids, or lead a normal life, living in bed day after day, takes a toll on you. Then things got worse.

Dr. Panic Disorder would prescribe me Xanax and anti-depressants on a visit. I finally broke down and took them. She would then deny me the next visit, sending me into horrific withdraws and sending me to the hospital. Then she would give them to me again. Repeat. The doctors at the hospital couldn't believe she was doing this. She was causing me to become sicker than I already was. I had to continue to see her, having no insurance, which I was working on getting government insurance, she was my only option, but the bitch was trying to kill me! She was the only one I could get my vertigo, nausea, and migraine meds from so, I had to go to her.

While waiting on my neurologist appointment, my symptoms were piling up and becoming stranger. It was affecting my vision, hearing. If I leaned over to pick something up, it burned behind my ears. Electrical shocks would shoot up the back of my skull, causing an instant migraine. No matter what test was run or what doctor I saw, they couldn't find anything wrong. Now, I was developing chronic pain. The doctors would stare at me as if I was some sort of hypochondriac. That's why they call it "invisible illness," morons! Just because you can't find it or see it doesn't mean it's not there. I was ready to wave the flag and throw in the towel. Come on, neurologist.

Chapter Thirty-Two
Hello Neurologist

The day of my neurologist appointment finally came. God, I was praying like hell for an answer. My body was so sick, and the pain was getting more severe. Still being unable to drive myself anywhere or even able to leave the house with no one, mom picked me up for the appointment, off we went on our journey, hoping for an answer to my medical mystery. We arrived at the I.U. Hospital in Indianapolis. We had to park in the parking garage, a challenging walk to get to the neurologist's office since my muscles were weak. We arrived, and I checked in. We were directed to sit in the waiting room until I was called back. What seemed like hours was only minutes. They were a hell of a lot faster than the damned doctor's office! The nurse called me back. Handing mom my coat, glancing down at her, "praying they tell me something," I told her.

"Me too," she answered.

Following the nurse back, she stuck me in a room and told me the neurologist would be in soon. Somehow, this time, I believed them. As I sat and waited, I peered around at the bright orange walls that were blurring my vision and triggering a headache. "Who the hell paints a neurologist office in bright ass colors," I thought to myself. "Dumbasses."

When the neurologist came in, I told him to note that his office should be a blander color.

He then told me, "You have signs of sensory overload. I am pretty sure you have it." Well, one thing down, a million to go, we were off to an excellent start.

Explaining every detail of everything I had been through from the beginning until the day I walked into his office (we were at over sixty symptoms by then), he made me go through all these tests. The best part he had seen this once before. Here it comes, I had Somatization Disorder. I released my breath until I heard the word "but."

"But what, doc?"

"But there is no cure. You have the worst-case I have seen going by your records. You're going to be hard to treat. It's sporadic. Most doctors know very little about it."

My mouth gaped, my eyes watered, keep laying it on me there, doc! He told me that most women that get it have a history of childhood sexual abuse! I'd like to shout out to the damn "pedophile." My body had been under so much stress all my life; the disease laid dormant. When I became stressed with the contractor, my body had all it could handle, went into fight or flight, and got stuck there. My body is always fighting itself.

It's attacking itself every minute of the day. It also caused my brain to backfire, and it no longer communicates with my body the way it should. It attacks everything in my body bones, nervous system, muscles, organs, immune system.

Whatever it wants to attack, it will. I am sick and in pain every day, and chances are, I will never get better. He told me to see a therapist. I gave him a "are you fucking kidding me" look. He said that there are most likely other things wrong with me, and it would help. Hating therapists and psychiatrists, I pretended to agree. He then sent me on my way with my diagnosis.

Walking out to the waiting room, I grabbed my coat from mom.

"What did he say? Did you get a diagnosis?"

"Yes. You will not believe this shit." I told her all about it as we trekked our way back to the parking garage. She was not a happy woman to know that the pedophile made me sick.

Lying in bed that night after getting my diagnosis and googling it on my phone at least a thousand times to see what I was dealing with, I had flashbacks of everything in my past, for as distant as I could remember, streaming through my head.

"This is some crazy shit," I mumbled to myself as I was thinking.

That son of a bitch took my childhood, my teen years, now my adulthood. Really?

I had told Corey about what the neurologist said, and for the first time in my life, I was speechless, and that is quite odd for me. I have a pretty big mouth just throwing that out there. I didn't gain a big mouth until my teen years, just clearing that up.

Me: "What a shitty life."

Some smartass: "At least you have one."

Me: "Bite me."

That's how I felt.

I laid there knowing I had made many mistakes in my life, but I was a kid. Grown-ups have no excuses.

Being bullied through elementary and middle school, then walking into a high school after blossoming over a summer, I realized I got out of control, finally getting attention from the popular kids, guys, and other kids outside of my average click of friends. It made me feel special. Like I was a "somebody." My body was blooming; the acne was disappearing. I could do my hair. Dress like the other kids.

I was finally coming out of my shell and showing that I had a personality that people enjoyed. I never took too much seriously, always joking, making people laugh, and I did have a heart. I never let my guard down, though. Learned from experience, you can't trust anyone, even if you wanted to.

Staring at the textured ceiling in the dark with thoughts still streaming like a river through my mind that dad spent fourteen-years of my life fucking up, it had been almost a year since I sustained this illness. Running my fingers through my dish blonde, long messy hair, that hadn't seen a brush in a few days, I thought, "Is this it? I'm only thirty-six. Will I grow old? Will this illness and pain cause my tragic demise? Man, this is some bullshit," I muttered, rolling onto my side.

I still had so much I wanted to do with my life to become an author, places to see, a social life, kids to raise and do life activities. I never slowed down. I would not survive living in a bed, being bedridden sick all the time. I was the President of the ADHD club! I didn't want to believe that this illness would never go away. There was no way it was going to last forever. Closing my eyes, somehow, I was determined to get through this and come out winning. The pedophile dealt me another lousy game to play checkmate; you bastard.

Chapter Thirty-Three
New Doctor And A Therapist, Kill Me Now, Please

My new government health insurance finally went into effect, and I could get into a new doctor. Bye, Doctor Panic Disorder. A friend recommended a top-notch internal medicine specialist so, I called his office and made an appointment. Eager to go, I would not explain to him my diagnosis, wanting to hear what he would come up with. It took two weeks to get in.

When I finally did, it was a meet and greet. What the hell? You mean a meet and take my damn copay? He wanted to see if we would be a good match, not even talking about my illness or pain. If it weren't for my mom driving, I probably would have found the nearest cliff, driving myself over the edge. Doctors were frustrating the hell out of me, sometimes more than being sick.

After making another appointment, I had to wait two more weeks. I was ready to rip the roof off the house. Having been sick for a year now, this was just becoming bullshit.

When I finally could get in to see Dr.

Please Help Me, (that's what we are going to call him, you will soon find out why), I explained to him what had been going on, all my symptoms, everything, well, at least when I could get a word in.

Dr. Please Help Me checked me over from head to toe, then ordered a bunch of tests. He came back with the words that I had heard before. The short, black hair Korean doctor I could barely understand rolled his chair up next to me.

"Lindsey, you have Somatization Disorder. Fibromyalgia too. Not a very good mix. I'll give you the number to a therapist's office. You need to see one. I'll be your doctor from now on. I will give you the medications you need." He rolled away from me, back to the computer, sending all my medications into the pharmacy.

"You can get sick like this from Post- Traumatic Stress Disorder," I asked with a shaky voice.

"Yes. It's rare, but you can. It depends on how severe the abuse or trauma. PTSD is trauma to the brain." He continued to type, squinting his eyes through his glasses.

"Dammit," I whispered, running both hands over my face in disbelief.

"Hmm? What did you say," Dr. Please Help Me asked?

Shaking my head, I said, "Oh, I said nothing."

He sent in my prescriptions, and I had to make a follow-up appointment to see him every thirty days. I hated going to the doctor. Barely went unless I had caught something I couldn't get rid of. Now, I was living in these damned offices. While I was there, Dr. Please Help Me explained that my belly bloating was from IBS or irritable bowel syndrome. He referred me to a GI doctor while I was there, too.

Great. More doctor's appointments. Most people WANT to go to the doctor when they are sick. I didn't. I was too sick and miserable to get out of bed and go, but I had no choice. Now, I wasn't only seeing an internal medicine specialist; I now had to call a GI doctor and a therapist. Therefore, pedophiles and rapists should be locked away in prison; not only do they commit horrendous crimes, they ruin their survivor's lives - our asses pay the price and do time.

Arriving home after picking up my medications, mom dropped me off because I still could not drive. My independence was something I lost and missed the most, too. Striding through the house and to my bedroom, I called and made an appointment with the therapy office, which was booked out a few weeks (go figure), and an appointment with the GI doctor for the following week. I had a lot of vomiting and burning in my chest and stomach, too, that I wanted him to check out. At least I didn't have to wait as long.

The GI doctor came in as I was waiting impatiently. He never did apologize for keeping me waiting for over an hour! We discussed my symptoms, and he made an appointment to do an endoscopy on me a few days later. By then, I had been picked and poked to death so much, I thought, "what the hell?"

The morning of the endoscopy arrived. Mom picked me up to take me to the hospital. My body trembled from a mixture of being nervous, I had never been under anesthesia before, and for some reason, I was always panicky when I left the house, calling it "my comfort zone."

Arriving at the hospital, they took me back and prepped me. It was over before I knew it. The GI doctor found nothing, just the fact that my brain wasn't communicating with my digestive system from the Somatization Disorder and IBS. Somatization Disorder is a tricky disease that can imitate ANYTHING. So, if it acts like a disease, I have to be tested for it. Unbelievable.

While making many appointments with different specialists, the disorder was causing more issues. From hearing and vision problems, appetite loss, muscle weakness, heat intolerance, cold intolerance, joint pain, muscle pain, chronic nausea, confusion, memory loss, GI problems, balance issues, troubles swallowing, and I would even become allergic to things and foods I was never allergic to before. I had over ninety-eight documented symptoms, and they were growing. Each day I was getting worse; I would never be normal again.

Chapter Thirty-Four
I Hate Therapists

It was time for my first therapy appointment. Three words; Kill me now. I hated therapists. "If you haven't gone through it, you don't know how I feel or shit about it. Your degree is like wet toilet paper to me. Not worth a shit." That is how I feel. Stepping into the office, my hair was in a messy ponytail, and my sweatshirt and sweatpants I had been wearing for days. This happens when you are so damned sick; you can't take care of yourself. By then, I was now fighting with a disability, who didn't think I was ill enough. My next step was a fucking coffin! I had been going on sick and in pain for almost two years now, and it was only progressing, making my life a living hell.

A therapist, Karen, called my name as I sat in my seat fidgeting. Following her back to her small little office with no windows, I had to look straight ahead. One of my symptoms was "sensory overload," and the pattern on the carpet was giving me vertigo, a headache, and nausea. Karen shut her door, sat down at her computer, getting right down to business. She questioned me about my medical history. The more I told her, the further I slumped down in my seat. Let the sweating, heart flipping, trembling, tunnel vision, nausea, damn near fainting begin! Speaking about it as much as I could, I could talk no more and cut her off. I cut her off rudely. She stopped the session, telling me I needed to see the medicine doctor next. I was a bit confused. What the fuck were they going to feed me now?

Strolling into the medicine nurse's office, she told me to take a seat. She searched her eyes through her computer; I was assuming reading everything the therapist had written. She then put me on an anti-depressant and Klonopin.

"Did that therapist lady diagnose me with something," I wondered?

"Yes, she did," she replied without peering away from her computer.

"And?"

"She didn't tell you?" She glanced over at me. She was probably very pale in her sixties, and her eyes bugged out like one of those bug-eyed fish you see at the aquariums. She was giving me the creeps. "You have a bipolar, borderline personality disorder, manic depression, severe depression, post-traumatic disorder, OCD, severe panic, and anxiety disorder with agoraphobia." She then turned back towards the computer.

"Great. I'm a freak." I rolled my eyes, taking a deep breath. She sent my medications through the computer, and off I went to make my follow up appointment. Mom was waiting in the car. I couldn't wait to tell her all about her daughter being a sociopath.

Between my trips to the doctor's offices and therapist's appointments, I was wearing down on top of fighting with my illness.

Fighting with a disability and the stress of not being able to help pay bills, do housework, and cook all the time was taking a significant toll on me, too. Everything was being taken away from me.

At the therapist's office, I had been through several therapists because of the dislike of the ones I had to see, and I could not stand the medicine nurse. She continued to give me medications that were causing me to become sicker with all the side effects. She would tell me to keep taking them even though they were killing me. I told her to fuck off. Thank God, she left, and a new nurse named Steve took her place. He understood me better and knew a little more about Somatization Disorder than anyone else, so we started from scratch and went through medications until we could find a combination that would not make me sicker than I already was. Somatization Disorder is classified as a mental illness. They use anti-depressants to help treat it. While trying to find the right medications, I laid low and never made another therapist appointment. See one to get your medicine. If they didn't ask me if I didn't see one, I sure as hell would not tell them. I'm a sneaky little shit. I just hoped it would last.

My failing health turned everything into constant chaos, so it seemed. I was running into one problem after another. I was having severe menstrual pain, found out I had endometriosis, had to have surgery. It took me longer than most women to heal because of my health. After a blood test, I was rushed to the cancer center and had to have a bone marrow biopsy done after being diagnosed with a blood disease called,

"Leukocytosis."

Usually, only people with Leukemia get it, but people with post-traumatic stress disorder can get it too, but it's rare. Very rare. It makes you tired all the time, and it can kill you. I have the best of luck. Dr. Quack convinced me to have a mammogram done. The cancer center called me. Are you kidding me? I had to go in and have my already pained boobs smashed all to hell again because they found a huge mass. They found out after hours of me cursing and apologizing for cursing, only to condemn also, as my boobs are being smashed and twisted in every direction known to man, that it was a massive cyst, but they have to keep an eye on it. Oh, I have breast density too. No shit? They also informed me that I was at an elevated risk for breast cancer. It figures.

My neurologist had to do a neuropathy test on one day. As the needles were being poked through my legs, blood seeping, I nearly clawed my way through the brick wall behind me, begging for mercy. He asked me to quiet down as I was crying out in pain.

Um, hello? I have PAIN condition. Like always, I ignored him, crying out through the rest of the torture. I wasn't sure how much more picking, poking, cutting open, and any other agony I could take! He performed a couple of MRI's on me because the Somatization Disorder was acting like it was Parkinson's Disease. We found white spots all over my brain from years of migraines, but nothing more, thank God.

At one of my visits with Steve, the medicine nurse, he caught me. I had to make an appointment with a therapist before I left, or he was going to have to stop my medications. We finally had found the right combination. I could function a little more, but I would never behave like a normal human being again. I will live sick and in pain every day for the rest of my life.

Sitting in the waiting room staring at the pattern of the carpet that gave me headaches, vertigo, and nausea every time I stepped into that God-forsaken therapist's office, a woman came out and called my name. She was as tall as me, about 5'7, short black hair, pretty, and didn't act as if she hated her job. She was nice. A little too friendly.

She was putty in my hands. Or so I thought. Thinking I could stroll into her office and shoot the shit, I sat down, and she turned on the computer.

"Crap" was the only word that came to mind. It's also my favorite word, in case you haven't noticed.

And she asked the question. "Tell me a little about your history." Taking a deep breath, giving a smartass gaze, I began. Throughout our session, I noticed, however, a straightforward thing. I didn't slump down in my seat or panic. This was a sign. A good sign. It meant I liked her. Wait, I enjoyed a therapist? It must have been the Somatization Disorder.

"So, Lindsey, how do you sleep at night?"

"What do you mean, Jenny?" I was confused by the question.

"Do you have flashbacks? Nightmares?" I nodded my head and locked eyes with her.

"Both." I shrugged a shoulder.

"Are you having a tough time sleeping?"

"Sometimes."

"Do you know why?"

I leaned forward. "You know when you are little, and you want to keep the boogeyman out, so you ask your parents if you can sleep with the door open?"

She peered at me as if I was freaking her out.

"Yes," she replied softly.

"I wanted to sleep with my door locked, to keep the boogeyman from coming in."

"How does that answer my question of how you sleep at night, Lindsey," she questioned with a shaky voice.

"Because sometimes I lay awake at night thinking about the horrible things that the boogeyman did to me." For the first time, I dropped my head down and cried. I cried so hard I couldn't catch my breath.

My dad was the monster, the pedophile, the rapist, and the GOD damned boogeyman. He made me mentally and physically sick. I felt so defeated. I had read so many books and watched so many TV shows of women like me that had happy endings. Where was my happy ending?

Chapter Thirty-Five
Betrayal, Secrets, And Strength

It's been six long years since I first got sick. Nothing has changed, just getting worse. Every day is a fight—a struggle. I fight with my diseases, my doctors, disability. I fight to keep bills paid with family and friends that deserted me once I became sick and useless to them. The people you are there for when you are healthy are no longer around when you are no longer used to them. It is a sad but true situation. Nobody helps you comes to visit or calls.

My kids grew up, well, the two oldest ones are now in their early twenties, and my daughter Katie gave me two precious grandsons. Most of the time, I can't enjoy them because I am too sick or in too much pain. As for Nick, he is growing up not knowing how a real mother should be. When I am not so bad, I take in each minute I spend with him as if it were my last. We go to the mall, Go-Kart track, out to eat, whatever he does.

It exhausts me when I do things like this, but I want to. It's my time with him, and I never know from one minute to the next if I will be plastered to the bed for days, weeks, or months riding out this God-awful disease. We did find out that I have

POTS syndrome, too, by the way. It's Postural Orthostatic Tachycardia. It explained my sudden blood pressure problems, along with my heart and near fainting.

My life is not every day, not that it never was, and some people tell me that I am strong, or how do I do it? I wasn't given a choice, and trust me, I am not as strong as they think. I have a lot of anger, depression, and frustration built up inside of me. Hate isn't even the word that I could use to describe what I feel for "the pedophile." I don't like to think he destroyed me, but he did. I think of suicide a lot. Daily. I can't stand living like this. It hurts. I am so sick all the time. But the only thing that stops me, my three kids, and two grandsons. I suffer terribly—more than I tell anyone. I feel like a burden because people have to help take care of me. There is so much guilt that comes with being chronically ill. If you don't "have it," you don't, "get it."

I continue to see the therapist that I like regularly and live at the doctor's offices. I don't even feel the needle anymore when they draw blood. Pretty sad, eh? However, I did discover a few things that were heartbreaking while I am still fighting disability.

One night, while sick in bed, my sister sent me a text message. She wanted to let me know that when she and her family took a trip to Florida; she visited the pedophile to introduce her family. She has been keeping in touch with him. What a kick to the face and the fucking heart. I spent years protecting her, allowing myself to be the target, swearing I would kill him if he ever touched her. She also remembered walking into the living room and seeing what he was doing to me while living in the apartment. Why are you telling me this now? She knew what he did to me, mom, and brother, and she visited the son of a bitch? I wanted to vomit. It made my stomach turn in knots.

How could you do that to your sister?

I also would like to send a shout out to the United States Army for the eighty-five- thousand-dollar check you wrote out to the pedophiler when you gave him that dishonorable discharge from the military, only because you wanted to wash your hands of him and the trouble he was causing.

Glad to see that abused children are your number one priority. Be proud.

My aunt and uncle came for a visit to the apartment, along with my young cousin, when we first moved back to Georgia. My aunt said they were there the whole time; they could sense something wasn't right with the pedophile. They perceived, right. And they were the only two that stood up for me in court the whole time. The rest of the family gets the middle finger salute and can go to hell.

They never kept in touch or cared enough to know how I was doing. Sometimes, the pedophile wins, and the survivor loses. The biggest mistake I ever made in my life was running away from Georgia's foster home. I should have stayed, toughed it out, had his ass locked up. Maybe they would have thrown away the key? Wishful thinking! But there is a special place for him when his time is up. He will forever burn in the depths of hell. Enjoy you son of a bitch.

Epilogue

I am now forty-two years old and still struggling to have a life for myself. I always have never given myself time to heal, although I am still seeing a therapist, and I am trying my best. Some people forgive, but they never forget. I refuse to do either. All the anger issues, troubles I caused in my marriage, and mental and physical illness result from a man who was supposed to love me, protect me from harm, not push my damage, and a lifetime of psychological and physical torture. He devoured every inch of my soul. Some days, I have more strength than others. Some days I want to give up because I am so sick, and the pain is terrible. It hurts to breathe. But I have three kids and two grandsons that motivate me to keep fighting and remain healthy. It is exhausting. Sometimes, I can be such a hypocrite. I tell others who have been through the same situations as I have to fight, stay positive and be healthy, and never let their attacker win when I have allowed mine to keep me from moving on and keeping me weak. I didn't have the support system like most victims do. Everything was a secret, shoved under the rug, and not to be discussed. Family members felt a sense of humiliation when it was brought up or spoken about.

There were even times where I was blamed.

I was blamed because I wanted to move back to Georgia to live with him, when all I wanted was to be a typical teenager, in a place that I called home, where I was with friends that I was growing up with. Kids are supposed to trust their parents. How was I supposed to know that mine was going to assault and brutally rape me sexually? Please don't assume that it's my fault. Why should I have to keep quiet about it? I did nothing wrong. I didn't commit the crime. If YOU are embarrassed, YOU are the problem. YOU are the reason women don't tell when something wrong happens to them. Victims should have a voice. We may have a voice. It's your story. You may tell your story. If you don't want to be in the story or the main character, don't misbehave. Young children grow up to be strong, independent adults someday.

The secrets you want us to keep, they won't be secrets forever. You will be exposed. Remember that. Take that into consideration before harming a child.

Because of my chronic illness and pain caused by my mental illnesses, it has put not only a strain on my life, my husband, and my family. Feeling like a burden and being sick all the time causes severe depression. I isolate myself to my room. Family and friends stop calling, visiting, texting, or ask how you are doing. They go on with their life. They don't think about you, and sometimes, I don't think they even care. It's a lonely place to be. I cry. I cry a lot.

I cry out for help when I am feeling suicidal. Nobody listens. If something terrible happens, I am the first to blame because I am the sick one and can't fight back. It's just some of the many things I have to go through daily.

"Dearly beloved...

We are gathered here today to get through this thing we call life..."

"So, when you call up that shrink in Beverly

Hills...you know the one? Dr. Everything'll be alright...

Instead of asking him how much time is left...

Ask him how much of your mind, baby..."

"Cause in this life

Things are much more challenging than in the afterworld...

In this life...

You're on your own..." - Prince

My name is A. L. Norton. I am Lindsey in this story.

Never be afraid to have a voice. Tell your story. And as I lay in bed every single day fighting for my life from this illness, blood disease, and the autoimmune diseases that I have now that can be fatal, I want everyone who suffers from PTSD or any type of mental illness to get treatment. I wish I did. I wish someone helped me. I wouldn't be lying here fighting for my life if I did.

I am getting worse by the day; doctors, specialists, surgeries, and so many medications. I take pills for everything. Complex Post Traumatic Disorder did a horrible job on me. I say I am no longer bitter, but in specific ways, I am. I try to stay positive. It's hard to when every day is a struggle to get out of bed. My body is slowly shutting down, but I remain strong and smile. Why do I smile after all I have been through.

I'll be damned if I let the bastard win.

This message is to all who have survived child abuse, domestic violence, or any other type of abuse. You will always have your good and bad days. Stay strong. Take care of yourself and never allow the dirty bastards them win. Please don't give them that satisfaction. They will have to meet their maker someday.

I am learning from it, and I have turned into the best person I can be, and so should you. My heart goes out to all of you. You've got this!

Thank you for reading my life story. Please be kind and leave me a kind review on Amazon or Goodreads or both, please.

To contact author A.L. Norton

Email- ambernorton4@aol.com

www.rainn.org

National suicide hotline

1-800-273-8255

Manufactured by Amazon.ca
Acheson, AB